Gentle Rain

Gentle Rain

Reflections on the Mercy of God

BITSY AYRES RUBSAMEN

BROADMAN
& HOLMAN
PUBLISHERS

Nashville, Tennessee

0-8054-5454-3
Published by Broadman & Holman Publishers,
Nashville, Tennessee
Acquisitions Editor: Vicki Crumpton
Page Design and Illustrations: Paul T. Gant Art and Design,
Nashville, Tennessee
Page Composition: Goeser & Goeser, Nashville, Tennessee

Dewey Decimal Classification: 242
Subject Heading: MEDITATIONS
Library of Congress Card Catalog Number: 97-44056

Unless otherwise stated all Scripture citation is from NASB, the New American Standard Bible, © the Lockman Foundation, 1960, 1962, 1963, 1968, 1971, 1972, 1973, 1975, 1977; used by permission. Other versions include Phillips, reprinted with permission of Macmillan Publishing Co., Inc. from J. B. Phillips: The New Testament in Modern English, revised edition, © J. B. Phillips 1958, 1960, 1972; The Message, the New Testament in Contemporary English, © 1993 by Eugene H. Peterson, published by NavPress, Colorado Springs, Colo.; NRSV; KJV, The King James Version; and The Jerusalem Bible, copyright © 1966 by Darton, Longman and Todd, Ltd. and Doubleday and Company, Inc. Used by permission of the publisher.

Library of Congress Cataloging-in-Publication Data
Rubsamen, Bitsy Ayres, 1936 –
Gentle rain : reflections on the mercy of God / Bitsy Ayres Rubsamen.
p. cm.
Includes bibliographical references.
ISBN 0-8054-5454-3 (hc)
1. Meditations.   I. Title.
BV4832.2.R79 1998
2421—dc21
                                                                97-44056
                                                                CIP
1 2 3 4 5 02 01 00 99 98

With deepest appreciation
and love I dedicate this book
to the two men who have
influenced my life the most.
To my husband, Rollins, for
his patience, kindness, and
steadfast love, who has
always given me the freedom
to be myself. And to my
brother Bobby (Robert Ayres,
Jr.), who has been my loving
encourager and witness to
the power of the Holy Spirit
through the works of service
he has done in the name of
Jesus Christ.

Table of Contents

Acknowledgments

I worked on this book for three years before I ever realized that I wanted to get serious about having it published. It was born out of the gentle prodding of Rev. Canon Mark Cannaday who, acting as my spiritual director, encouraged me to journal during my prayer time. I have a heart full of gratitude for his leading me into this endeavor.

There have been others who recognized my gift of writing and sought to encourage me as well. A thousand thank-yous to Betsy Slater Dudley, who has been a source of affirmation for me over the past twenty years. Also, heartfelt thanks must go to Deborah Hanus who instructed me in the art of spiritual direction, and who, upon recognizing my gift of words would say to me, "Say it, 'I am a writer.'" My deep appreciation goes to Rev. Clifford Waller, my dear friend and mentor, who has been eager to see parts of "my story" told; and to Merry Molteni who, in listening to me read my stories, has helped me to recognize my own voice; to Paula D'Arcy, my new friend and fellow writer who came alongside of me just because she wanted to get to know me, and who kept telling me that some day I would get published; and to Kathleen Davis Niendorff, my agent, who pushed and prodded out of me the best that I thought I could give. She has become so much more; she is a dear and loving friend. And last of all, I want to acknowledge my editor Vicki Crumpton, into whose capable hands my manuscript landed, and express my gratitude to all of the other caring people at Broadman & Holman Publishers.

Thank you all for helping to bring this book to life.

Introduction

As a moth
is drawn into the light,
so am I,
and the flame of Your
Eternal Light
touches my heart
and singes
the open wounds
which seem slow
to heal,
bleeding still,
yet allowing me
to feel
the hurt of others
who brush against my life.

Upon Your flame
I focus my eyes
and there,
drawn upon my mind,
an image,
a knowing that is
Ancient Truth,
that You are Life Eternal,
healing,
loving,
owning me,
because I accepted You,
embraced You,
and allowed You
to shine
the flame of Your Eternal Love
upon my wounded heart.

What do you experience when you reach out and touch a flame? No matter how quickly you withdraw your finger, it will still burn a little. And if you leave it there for very long, it will become painfully blistered and possibly scarred. I was touched, burned, and even scarred in a beautiful way by the flame of God's merciful love when I experienced my conversion in Jesus Christ.

I grew up in the country on a farm complete with the usual assortment of barnyard animals. My two older brothers raised Hereford cattle and sheep to show at livestock exhibitions. My after-school hours were spent playing with these animal friends, visiting the vegetable garden, or roaming through the pastures with my sister. I experienced a wonderful sense of freedom, and I loved it. In fact, I much preferred being there than any other place. I now know that as a child, I recognized God as a benevolent father whose creation gave me a deep sense of wonder and happiness. But I believe that my beloved haven also gave birth to a sense of insecurity, for it kept me distanced from daily social activities with neighborhood friends.

As I began to look back over my life, paying attention to the more significant experiences, I could see areas in which I needed understanding. I was unaware that these insecurities had played a role in my life, because I kept them hidden from others and myself. I believe they had wounded me, but it wasn't until I made a commitment to a personal relationship with Christ as Lord of my life that I recognized this. I slowly began to view things differently. I began to trust God, the Heavenly Father, because of the promises found in the Holy Scriptures granted me through the gift of His Son. I thought that if I could be healed from the belief that I was an inferior woman not called to any particular purpose, then perhaps I could also help others toward wholeness and significance of purpose as well.

So I acknowledged my sense of "woundedness" and began to count it as blessing, sharing with others what I was learning. I focused on my "light" side, sensitivity and compassion, instead of my "shadow" side's crippling weakness and insecurity. I found St. Paul's words Romans, chapter 12, challenging me: "Do not be conformed to this world, but be transformed by the renewal of your mind, that you may prove what the will of God is, that which is good and acceptable and perfect." I wondered how one's mind became truly transformed.

I began to discover that my life experiences gave interpretation to Holy Scripture. God's Word actually took on a keener sense of truth when anchored in real situations, and His incredible mercy became a constant companion to my thoughts. Those wonderful words of William Shakespeare in *The Merchant of Venice* Act IV came as revelation, repeatedly washing my adult mind with its rich ring of truth, a truth unattainable to the high school girl who memorized them years ago:

> The quality of mercy is not strained;
> It droppeth as the gentle rain from heaven
> Upon the place beneath. It is twice blest;
> It blesseth him that gives and him that takes.
> 'Tis mightiest in the mightiest; it becomes
> The throned monarch better than his crown.
> His sceptre shows the force of temporal power.
> The attribute to awe and majesty,
> Wherein doth sit the dread and fear of kings;
> But mercy is above this scept'red sway;
> It is enthroned in the hearts of kings;
> It is an attribute to God himself,
> And earthly power doth then show likest God's
> When mercy seasons justice.

This same mercy has the power to transform not just the mightiest of monarchs but also the lowliest of men and women into their highest potential.

The reflections in these pages are very honest, make me vulnerable to you, but I am convinced that through this openness, you too may come to a deeper sense of wholeness. I recently heard about a on the mission field in Zaire who said: "In order to heal others, you must forget about yourself." What helps me to forget about myself is deep self-knowledge and acceptance. Having that awareness has enabled me to understand the gentle healing that God in His unfathomable mercy yearns to rain down on all His children.

transformed
by His Mercy

Come!

Can you hear it?
It romances me, calls me
to step differently than before.
I know there are others who hear its beat,
and march without hesitation
into the rhythm of life.
I'm cautious,
yet that beat entices.

Who is the drummer,
the one who cradles the drum between strong limbs?
The one who beats an unnatural rhythm
for natural man?
That beat is calling me to move this way and that.
Awkwardly at first,
then trusting in its rhythm,
comfortable in the steps I take.

More assured,
I look toward
the One who plays.
I move unafraid.
I know now.
The drum which calls
is in the hands
of Christ!

 friend of mine once told me about a production of the British Broadcasting Corporation that portrayed Jesus Christ in the gospel of Mark as being a man of very high energy who was urgent in His call and in His teaching.

As I think about a "high-energy" Christ, I smile because I am married to a high-energy person. Rollins always amazes me by the capacity he has to accomplish the things he loves to do. There are not many obstacles that can hold that good man down! Friends respond to his spontaneity and good nature. The twinkle in his eye reflects the ease with which he faces most of life's situations. There's power in that personality—a certain charm which draws and coaxes others who are in his presence.

So as I think about a high-energy Christ, I can appreciate what it was like to be His friend. A picture comes to mind of an encourager with a bountiful supply of charisma and mystery as well. Had we been privileged to overhear Him speaking to His followers we might have heard Him say:

> Come quickly! Sit down and be quiet. I will bless your efforts. Never fear. I love your obedience in the things that you do for Me. But now I want to show you more, perhaps the most important part about our journey towards My Father's Kingdom. So stay close. Hold My hand, as we walk along a different path—one on which you've never been before. You must trust Me to lead you. Just follow. Trust and listen, as I lead you into silence. There lies peace and rest for your soul.

> Did I hear you say, wearily, how hard it is to be still? That's because you've been running so long. I'm here to teach you a new and different way. Just listen to the silence and trust it. Although you will travel through dark nights, I will never leave You. I will always be with you. I want to lead you further into greener pastures and peaceful valleys.

> So come! Follow Me! I have incredible joy in store for you, and when you leave the silence and return to the work-a-day world, many will come to you, and they will know by the radiance of your face and the twinkle in

your eye that you have been touched by something other. And they will question you. Then, you can tell them about Me.

I like that picture of Christ. It is easy for me to see Him that way. It is because I have seen Christ in Rollins. The love he's given me through the years has nurtured and coaxed me in to being more fully who I am. That kind of love leaves its mark. People can tell, because it shows.

"Come, follow Me."
John 2:43
The Message

A New Creature

Why is it so difficult
just to be
that which You created?
To think Your thoughts,
to do Your will.

Why am I deceived?
Man's needs seem so complex,
yet
You call me
to come with heavy burdens
and leave them
at Your cross.
And, like magic,
conversion happens,
bringing tears of pain,
relief!

Your magic,
Majestic Magic!
You promised to work its spell
within my tired and worn-out soul.
Like springs of living water
splashing down,
down,
down
into all of my being.

When did I ever think
I could
be
without You?

The moment of conversion for Christ's disciples happened very quickly. We are told that Andrew met Him first, then ran and told Peter about Him.

Then Jesus walked by one day. Andrew and Peter were fishing. They stopped and listened to this man, and He said, "Follow Me." From that moment on, their lives were changed. The same

thing happened to Zebedee's two sons, James and John
(Matt. 4:21–22); only this time, we are told, these brothers left
not only their fishing boat but their father as well.

What happens to a person at conversion that causes such a
dramatic change? Many people take offense at the thought of
one single act of transformation; others are highly skeptical and
give no credence whatsoever to the experience. Through the
years I have learned that we don't all come into a relationship
with the living God the same way. For me, however, the immedi-
acy was real, maybe even similar to that of the fishermen who
sailed the waters of the Galilean Sea.

My conversion took place in 1971 on the Sunday morning of
a Faith Alive weekend being held at our church. Such a weekend
involves a team of lay visitors who have been invited by the
church to share with others what their personal relationship
with Christ means to them. I went to church that morning as
usual with my family. I left there a new person. Paul describes it
this way: "Therefore if any man is in Christ, he is a new creature;
the old things passed away; behold, new things have come" (2
Cor. 5:17).

I was sitting with my husband listening to one of our visitors
tell his story about the power of Christ in his life. When he finished speaking, the congregation was given the opportunity to
go forward for an altar call—an unusual moment in the usually
rather formal liturgical setting of the Episcopal church in those
years. I went and found myself kneeling with a friend who
prayed for me. In an instant, I was changed! To my astonishment,
I began sobbing uncontrollably. At that moment, Christ's Spirit
came to life in me. The tears of my new birth flowed through the
rest of the service, leaving my husband feeling helpless as he
tried to console me. I sensed that he was embarrassed for me as
well as for himself, because, for him as for many men, tears are
often hard to deal with.

I was changed in an instant. I began to respond to things differently. A new creature inside my familiar body had come to
life. I had suddenly begun to live in a whole new realm of reality.

Even though Christ called me to follow Him, He did not call me to drop everything I was doing nor to leave my family. Christ's call might have been easier for those fishermen than for me; because when I began to change, it caused some misunderstandings among my family and friends. The period of adjustment that followed was long and sometimes difficult because it affected the whole family. I know there were times when they wished that they had their old, familiar wife and mother back! Our daughter Ann, who was taking driving lessons, was so preoccupied with what happened to me that one day she announced to the car full of students and her instructor that her mother had "gone ape over Jesus"!

Certain activities no longer held my interest. I had no distaste for them; I just had a new and hearty appetite to be among Christians who could help nurture this newly reborn creature through Bible study and prayer. Christian fellowship took on a new and deeper meaning. I couldn't seem to get my fill, and yet I was constrained by deep commitments to my family and to my community.

Conversion takes place, but life and its hardships go on. When we are reborn we are not transported out of this world into a heavenly realm. I like to think that if I could give Christ a theme song it would be that country tune that was popular a few years ago, whose first line says, "I beg your pardon, I never promised you a rose garden."

No, He certainly didn't promise that. But I believe that He gives us the grace to cultivate beauty wherever we live. He calls us to be who we are, living in our little corners of the world, only now with a major difference—to live there for Him!

And they immediately left the nets, and followed Him.
Matthew 4:20

George

A kiss was placed on Frog's green and moistened cheek,
and he became a prince
bedecked in gaudy splendor,
with charming ways,
so well known by man.
His handsome ways spoke
of temporal hope.
A woman's kiss worked well,
the story tells.

A kiss was placed on Man's curved and softened cheek,
and he became
transformed
into the likeness of his Beloved.
Dressed not as prince,
nay,
grander still!
Its splendor worked magic
on his soul.

We love our human kisses, same as Frog.
To be a prince,
to charm the world,
but,
to be kissed by God
is our deepest need.
That kiss
transforms
our restless heart and soul.

 s I drove to George's house for a visit the other day, I reflected upon this wonderful friend who has been Christ to many people over the past twenty-five years due to the transforming power of God's love in his life.

"Jesus was always real to me," George told me as we sat in front of the picture window of his living room. "But for many years, I never let Him grow up," he continued. "He was just a baby. I kept Him wrapped in swaddling clothes in the manger. I never experienced His power. He was just a little guy, and, although I knew about His death and resurrection, He just never grew up. I guess you could say that my Christianity was stuck in infancy.

"It really wasn't until 1971, when I was forty-two years old, after the Faith Alive experience at St. Mark's that I really allowed Jesus to grow up," he continued. "It has been a slow process, but as I've allowed Him to mature, I have grown up too.

"Just before that life-changing weekend, I had started attending St. Mark's because I had met a woman who was a member of that parish, and we planned to be married there. The date had been set, but a few weeks before our wedding day she went off to Mexico and married another man. That was a very painful experience for me. I nearly lost it.

"I went down to tell the priest the wedding was off. He said, 'George, I want you to remember three things: first, God loves you; second, I love you; and third, come to church on Sunday.' I believe that was the first time that I really heard that God loved me, and so I began to attend church there. I went every Sunday."

George paused for a few moments for reflection as he looked out the window to the backyard. Then he continued, "A year later at a Faith Alive reunion, I met Merry. A short time later we married. One night as I lay down to go to sleep, God spoke to me saying, 'George, you are going to die.' That voice was just as clear to me as any I had ever heard. I sat straight up in bed. I was so shaken that I woke Merry. It disturbed me very much. I'd finally reached a point in my life that I really didn't want to die. Life had taken on new meaning.

"The next morning, still shaken, I telephoned a close friend of mine and asked him to meet me for lunch. I was surprised when both he and his wife came into the drugstore's little corner lunchroom. I hadn't planned to share my anxiety in front of his wife, too, but before I could change my mind about the whole idea, my friends sat down across the little table from me and asked me what was happening.

"So I told them what God had said. They turned to one another and began to smile. Frankly, I didn't see anything amusing. Then my friend's wife said, 'George, God is telling you that the old George is going to die and a new George is going to be born.'"

Once again George paused to reflect. As we sat in silence, I remembered hearing this story when Rollins and I first came to know George. It was good to hear him retell it himself. He began talking about his terrible temper, how, when angry, he used to slam his fist into walls and doors.

"My friend and his wife were right. It wasn't easy, but I began to change. I realized I'd never taken responsibility for my anger. I'd always blamed someone else or something else for making me mad. And I began to understand the hurt I'd caused others and myself.

"Another friend taught me how to master the rage. At his suggestion, every morning while I shave before the mirror, I look myself in the eye and say, 'No one can make me mad today.' It sounds simple, but it works. Oh sure, when my guard is down, somebody will push my button. I guess coals are still there blanketed under layers of ashes, but as the years have gone by and the ashes have grown deeper, the fire doesn't burn as hot anymore. What the priest told me about God's loving me became real through the love and understanding given to me by so many friends."

As I drove away from George's house that day, I thought about the change that takes place when a person experiences the love of God through others. George was healed of a broken heart by the love he received from his new church community and his marriage to Merry. He was also healed of his anger. I believe that the transforming kiss of God sometimes bestowed by our brothers and sisters in Christ can make people grow both strong and gentle in the assurance of their being beloved. I don't suppose it's really so different from the kiss that changed the frog into a prince—except that God's kiss is everlasting and has the power to change lives.

For you have died and your life is hidden
with Christ in God.
Colossians 3:3

The Banquet

I strive to claim charitable ways.
How empty!
I cannot attain the blessedness of God
until my heart gives way to hunger and thirst,
and I go impoverished,
to the banquet table of Christ.

There He will feed me:
Flesh which gives flesh to my will;
He will quench my thirst.
Blood poured out
brings life
to my soul.

The banquet hall awaits. I go.
Yes, slowly I go.
I know He'll wait, yet I must not tarry.
Traps are set to snare
when I linger too long
at empty tables.

ust before lunch one day during a week-long retreat, the retreat leader asked us, as a form of grace, to look at our plates and consider all that had died to nourish us. This, for me, was a new and startling way to contemplate the cycle of death and rebirth.

"I tell you, most solemnly, unless a wheat grain falls on the ground and dies, it remains only a single grain; but if it dies, it yields a rich harvest" (John 12:24, *The Jerusalem Bible*).

And truly, in order to bring new life to others, I must continually be dying to self. I don't do this well most of the time. Some things are easier to let die than others. But it is usually those hard ones, when dead and buried, that give greater nourishment.

My vanity and pride were dealt a healthy blow one Sunday morning while I was sharing my life with Christ to a church packed with people. When I finished my story and began to return to my seat, I fell down the chancel steps into an awkward heap. I found myself apologizing to the minister as he hurried over to give me a hand and to my husband who came quickly to assist me back to the pew. Once seated, I remembered the injunction to give thanks in all things, so I knelt and said prayerfully, "Thank you, Lord, I think!"

After the service was over, many people thanked me for what I had shared. Others expressed their embarrassment for me over my fall. But one of the last people to approach me was a shy, plump young woman who took me aside and said something like this: "You know, I'm glad you fell. I mean, I've been watching you all weekend. You're so dainty and petite, and I've always been awkward and clumsy. So when you fell down that step, it made me feel better."

It was at that point that I really accepted that awful moment of embarrassment and offered to God a truly grateful heart. This business of having to die to our many forms of self is serious indeed. But I can do it, if I choose to. I believe I have far more to give to another than my verbal witness of Christ in my life. I want to show them, too, even at the expense of vanity and pride that, at the bottom line, we are all more alike than we are different.

O Lord, I close my eyes and see
my mother's face upon my own.
Crying.
Dying.
Must I die too?
Now? So soon, yet
a certain death must claim me
to transform and resurrect
the creature You have placed within.
The one You knew long before I knew: Myself!

The Taste of More

How patient You must have been to wait
for the unfolding of Creation!
The whole, big picture complete!
Each star in place.
Each grain of sand set
in its appointed space.

What was it like to know
You could create any which way You chose,
to delight Your fancy
and to think of delighting mine?
Creation's purpose, to stir my heart
and sustain my soul with joy.

Her beauty never changes.
Only my desire to own her
and to claim her as my inheritance.
To nurture and to love her as You planned
that I should do.

Place on my heart, O Lord,
a picture of Your glory
that shines through every branch and blade I see.
I yearn to share that which I know
has left an imprint on my soul.

ncle Henry was an old man who worked for our family when I was a little girl. In many ways, he was like a parent to me because he taught me much about the wonder of creation and the goodness of the simple things of life.

Even though he walked with a limp and depended on a cane, he stayed busy doing chores around our country home, never allowing his rheumatism to prevent him from completing a task.

One of his jobs was the care of the victory garden between our house and the old barn. I used to spend hours with him there and can still remember the fascination I had each time he would let me pull at the fernlike green top of a carrot until it loosened from the earth and revealed its brilliant orange root.

I can also boast that, because of Uncle Henry, I learned how to eat chicken feet. We raised chickens, and Sunday lunch with fried chicken was a family tradition. After we had finished eating and I was excused from the table, I would wander into the kitchen to talk with him while he ate. I especially liked to watch him chew on the chicken feet. On more than one occasion, he shared a foot with me, telling me just to chew a little of this part or that part, but not the claws! Can you imagine? Oh, I remember it as wonderful fun!

But the thing he seemed to like most about those chicken dinners was the gravy the cook always prepared to go with the mashed potatoes.

"Know what this tastes like?" Uncle Henry would say with a twinkle in his eye, as he rose up from the kitchen table and walked to the stove to fetch another spoonful of gravy. "This tastes like more."

I'm thankful that I've never forgotten Uncle Henry and his love for the simple pleasures of life. Not once did I hear him complain. When World War II was raging and the essentials of life were being rationed, he taught me to savor the goodness of things taken for granted.

On the steps of the school I attended as a young girl were engraved the words: "Teach Us Delight In Simple Things." If I remember anything of my school experience, it has been those words. God has filled my life with an abundance of goodness, and He generously places it where I can experience it. The choice is mine.

Can I be one who has the eyes to see the holy in the ordinary? Can I love the things that taste like more?

And God saw all that He had made, and
behold, it was very good.
Genesis 1:31

Hearing Voices

O Light adoring, You search my soul
to shine upon those parts which hide.
Keep searching!
Don't stop!
I fear you'll leave,
and then alone,
my thoughts
will be condemning.

The words of a prayer I read a few years ago
touched a truth in me. Entitled
"A Prayer to Own Your Beauty," it reads:

O God,
help me
to believe
the truth about myself
no matter how beautiful it is![1]

he first time I read it, I fought back tears. I had to ask
myself what it was within me that reacted so violently
to it, and why was I fighting against the truth within
myself. I have struggled with my tendency to ignore the beauty,
choosing to look at the ugly side instead. I wanted to celebrate
the beauty within, but I knew that I needed the transforming
power of the light of Christ in order to do so. I needed His power

to turn my dark side into light.

It is sometimes the enemy whose voice we hear. He seeks to nurture our fears, to discourage our faith in the act of transformation. Yet the words of Scripture tell us that Christ told many stories about victory through transformation.

Transformation started for me when I began to seek to renew my mind by accepting the truth. It meant that I needed to think differently about myself and to see that face that looks back at me in the mirror in a new way. Perhaps I needed to think about and look at others differently as well. I know that it has sometimes been easy for me to be critical of others because I have been mostly unconsciously critical of myself.

But Jesus said: "Don't pick on people, jump on their failures, criticize their faults—unless, of course, you want the same treatment. That critical spirit has a way of boomeranging" (Matt. 7:1–2, The Message).

Jesus Christ is very direct here. He warns us that as we judge others, we will be judged in return. Was my ugly, dark side the "other" I judged the most? But within the light of His Truth, reality is revealed. Often the voice of the one who judges has first experienced the pain of judgment by others. I can pity the Pharisees! They were burdened down with more than heavy robes, tassels, and phylacteries! They had been judged as well. And as their fingers pointed and their words were hurled in judgment, the Truth was called a lie.

I heard someone describe Jesus as the "Incendiary Christ"— on fire with a burning love for humanity such as the world had never witnessed before. Some may think that such love burned out when He died on the cross for our sins. But don't you believe that for a minute! It didn't. His fire still burns. The power that resurrected our beloved Savior is the same power given to those who choose Him. It is resurrection power—power that cleanses us and heals our self-inflicted wounds.

Thus, I have learned that there is no room in my mind for the enemy's voice, even though he may speak through those I know and even love.

Jesus said to him, "I am the way, and the truth, and the life."
John 14:6

Heart Knowledge

Knowing came fluttering by.
A sight of black and gold
caught in midair,
instantaneous,
yet prolonged enough
for Truth to usher in
a radiance of Peace and Hope.

As a newborn babe,
anticipation cradled me in its open hands
in what my heart yearned to believe.
Resurrection!
Unbound from the old.
Transformed!
Now all newfangled and glorious!

Oh yes, You told us it would be so.
"Whoever believes in Me,
I shall raise up on the last day."

 have given up limiting God's speech and action to ways acceptable only to our Western minds. A few weeks after my father's death, haunted by uncertainty of his salvation, I asked, "Where is he, God?" I knew what I hoped for, but doubt intensified my grief over his death.

21

Daddy was not a churchman; that is, truth to tell, he really didn't like church. He had been baptized and confirmed; he was a forgiving, sweet, and loving father to me, one who walked through life with the doubts, fears, and uncertainties we all face along the journey.

But as I struggled with the pain of uncertainty of his salvation one afternoon, I walked through the kitchen door, down the back steps, and out into our backyard. Suddenly a butterfly flew directly in my path about waist high, causing me to stop abruptly so as not to bump into it. Briefly, it hovered there, in hummingbird fashion, as if begging for my attention. I felt a presence, undeniable and unexplainable, speaking to me as I stood immobilized before this tiny messenger, this living symbol of resurrection. As soon as the message was received by my heart, the butterfly darted off. The pain of uncertainty vanished with that little creature, and I was filled by a deep sense of peace about my father.

It was as if Joan of Arc were whispering her words into my mind: "God speaks to us in ways we can understand." She experienced wonderful revelations through her God-given imagination and defended her actions as based on this inspiration, for which she was burned at the stake. Can He not speak to me also in that way? Sometimes the healing of my faith comes when I open the doors of my inner knowing and allow His Spirit to gently blow away my doubt. So who am I to forbid Him the freedom to reveal Himself in any way He may choose? I wonder if He is ever frustrated by a shallow and narrow faith that prevents the mystery of His incredible love from going deeper, filling the void that keeps us from being whole.

But there's far more to life for us. We're citizens of high heaven! We're waiting the arrival of the

*Savior, the Master, Jesus Christ, who will transform
our earthy bodies into glorious bodies like his
own. He'll make us beautiful and whole with the
same powerful skill by which he is
putting everything as it should be,
under and around him.*
Philippians 3:20–21, *The Message*

Transforming Waters

You bid me
"Step forward."
Waves as tall as towers stand,
motionless on either side.
And yet I seem frozen,
paralyzed!

Why, O Lord,
can't I step forward
knowing
that it's by
Your hand
my path is marked?

 he tragedy of the Oklahoma City federal building bombing in the spring of 1995 left an impact on the spirit of the American people. The destruction of life and property not only marred the beauty of a strong and vital city, but the trust and faith of millions throughout our country as well.

Scenes of destruction and heartbreak still flash through my mind. Thousands of families will never be the same; only memories of what it was like to have a mother, husband, son, or daughter will remain. To be sure, a tragedy of this magnitude will impact the national consciousness for decades to come.

Yet I have to believe that something beautiful continues to rise up out of all the twisted steel and broken bodies. It began to happen when people just like you and me were drawn out of their own personal lives with their own problems into the lives of fellow citizens in order to do whatever they could to comfort and aid those who had lost so much. It was evidenced in pictures of the rescue teams who walked purposefully through those towering walls of destruction, risking their own lives, in order to dig through rubble in search of life. Workers toiled feverishly to find, and raise up out of the ruins, hope that would bring a nation back to life. They were not paralyzed by fear but motivated by a love stronger than the hate that caused such pain.

God calls me to live above the level of mediocrity as He releases me from the paralysis of my fear. Yesterday I listened to the pain of a stranger who sought my help. And beyond her words, I heard a desperate cry for me to rescue her from a sense of craziness as she anguished at the thought of the death of her marriage. Momentarily, old fears of inadequacy came rushing in on me like a tidal wave. In the past, the timid Bitsy would have recoiled—graciously, of course, on the outside—and walked away. How could I begin to help someone in such pain? I could not have helped her then, because I myself had not yet become acquainted with the power of God's love.

But as I listened to her fearful voice, I could hear the strong voice of my own faith and hope rising up from deep within, speaking the truth through gentle and reassuring words. And in my mind's eye I watched her fear begin to crumble in submission to the strong towers of God's transforming, healing love.

"Behold, I have given you authority to tread upon serpents and scorpions, and over all the power of the enemy, and nothing shall injure you."
Luke 10:19

healing
through His Mercy

Life-Giver

Lifeless days file by
empty of a shared love.
Death claimed once cherished dreams
and beauty faded
as night's shadow snuffed out
the light.

O Christ, I feel the pain.
How can I help
revive a dying soul?
"Look beyond your fears, My friend.
Risk to love
with the love I give.
I'll be your strength.
I'll be your gentleness.
I'll be that kiss of life.
He who now seems dead will
rise and walk again."

 he mission and purpose of the church are described in many ways, and in different lives it takes different forms of expression, but I like to think of it in this way: the purpose and mission in life of a person called to live under the influence of Jesus is to raise the dead."[2]

My mind whirled as I read those words given in a meditation by Rev. Theodore Parker Ferris to a gathering of women in San

Francisco in 1949. I realized he was also speaking to me today.

It's one thing to be an instrument of healing, but raising the dead is an entirely different issue! How can I? True, Christ asks of us what He asked of His disciples. Not only did He ask them to heal the sick and feed the poor, but raise the dead as well. And often because of their lack of faith, they ran to get Him to do the job. It's no different with me. I will often defer to someone else, perhaps someone older or wiser.

The tragedy that befell longtime friends of mine several years ago changed the course of their lives forever. Their adult son was killed. I remember how I felt when I received the news of his death. My whole body seemed to wrench in disbelief and pain. I could not believe it had happened to someone who had, as a child, spent so many hours with our family. Our lives had been intertwined. Even though time and distance had separated us, I felt numbed by the thought of his senseless death and the excruciating pain his family was feeling. They were left with only memories of the life and love they had with him. Having never experienced the loss of a child, I knew I was incapable of really knowing how they felt; but having lost my sister through a tragic accident, I had been witness to my own parents' grief. I knew the process of healing from this grief would seem unending.

Love rushed me to his grieving parents' home. And yet there was a certain anxiety I felt as I entered the front door, almost as if I were intruding upon their grief. I felt this because I felt so inadequate. I began to question myself, wondering what I could possibly say that would comfort. I felt that any attempts to express my love would seem awkward. I now realize that my own self-centeredness had me preoccupied with thoughts about how I would be received instead of concentrating on giving them the love I had to give.

As time has passed, it has become evident that my visits have been times for listening as my friend pours out her pain. God calls us to be available to others who are hurting, blinded by whatever pain may be in their lives, and to help them discover for themselves the freedom and truth of Christ's redeeming love which will bring them new life. He calls us to be available as faith healers.

Brennan Manning speaks of fear as a barrier to the healing of those who are dying for lack of love: "Each of us pays a heavy price for our fear of falling flat on our face. It assures the progressive narrowing of our personalities and prevents exploration and experimentation. As we get older we do only the things we do well. There is not growth in Christ Jesus without some difficulty and fumbling."[3]

I can close my eyes to the pain of death and be unwilling to risk. But Christ calls me to open my eyes so that I can see. He gave me a life to give back to Him which is tailor-made, just for me. When I am willing to be obedient to His call and abide in Him; when my trust in Him overrides my fear of failure; then I find that I can indeed help to bring others back from the grip of illness or an earthly and temporal death into life in eternal light. Others helped me to be healed and to live. They took a leap of faith and, like Lazarus, I was unbound and set free. And so the business of prayer and watching with Him must be the order of my days.

"Keep watching and praying, that you may not enter into temptation."
Matthew 26:41

"Heal the sick, raise the dead, cleanse the lepers, cast out demons; freely you received, freely give."
Matthew 10:8

Consider the Good Part

To the image of You
I run.
Meet me, please,
in my hour of quiet.

Allow me to treat You
as a friend.
For You are friend
to all who call Your name.

Sit by my side
and listen.
Those things I share with no one
I bring to You.

Smile at me
Your blessed assurance,
and cause my heart
to rest.

Then down through transforming waters
as if alone I'm drawn,
deeper
down I go,
following
where You seem to have gone.

Somewhere, but nowhere.
There!
In silence, my greatest need uncovered,
I cry, "Lord Jesus, in Your mercy,
pray me."

 sit in the quiet, asking God to speak to me in ways I can understand. Silence comes at first, followed by the voice of Truth:

Be still and rest in My presence. Listen to your heart.

I know what lies inside: unspoken hurts and disappointments as well as your desires. They are projected by your words and actions. Do you recognize them?

I want you to stop your busyness and learn what My presence can bring to you. Learn that it can be a greater gift toward fulfillment than all that you feel you should do. Part of being present to others means, first of all, being present to Me. I am the guest who has come today.

I have often filled my days with so much I think must be done. The doing cushions me from things I'd rather not face. It keeps me unaware, and I become deaf to the voice of God. Yet I have come to realize that busyness can be the enemy's tool just like idleness can. It prepares the way for confusion to enter my mind, and with it a sense of paralyzing doubt. Sometimes insecurities appear as well, fed by negative thoughts, not only about myself, but about others as well. This is destructive power that's not easy to live with. I recognize the damage it can do, and I stand in disbelief at the pain I inflict upon myself! Surely, if I'm capable of such self-destructiveness, my critical thought of others could hurt them as well.

In the stillness, God reveals the ugly, dark areas within. That is where He'd have me be busy—cleaning up my inner household.

In Richard Foster's popular book *Celebration of Discipline: The Path to Spiritual Growth,* he makes a strong case for the practice of contemplative moments of solitude: "The fruit of solitude is increased sensitivity and compassion for others. There comes a new freedom to be with people. There is new attentiveness to their needs, new responsiveness to their hurts."[4]

Paul's words bear repeating: "And not be conformed to this world, but be transformed by the renewing of your mind, that you may prove what the will of God is, that which is good and acceptable and perfect" (Rom. 12:2).

The renewal of the mind brings healing to the soul. Therefore, hope lies in the quiet of God's presence, and it waits for me to embrace it! Action must follow contemplative moments, but action must wait its turn. For me, there is no choice.

"Martha, Martha, you are worried and bothered about so many things; but only a few things are necessary, really only one, for Mary has chosen the good part, which shall not be taken away from her."
Luke 10:41–42

Rats and Living Water

Thirst-quenching, life-giving,

clear and cool,

or so it may appear.

But Jesus knows those ills which spoil

that which seems so pure.

To drink from anything less

than the well of Living Water

will bring death.

aving grown up a country girl, I have fond memories
of wonderfully funny events that happened during
those years, like the day of the rat circus! I was about
six years old. This particular day my two older brothers were
taking pot shots at rats on the electrical wires that connected
our house, the old green wooden water tower, and the barn on

the other side. To me, the agility of those rats was just as amazing as any high-wire act I had ever seen! I can close my eyes and still see the unending line of gray, fat-bodied creatures teetering precariously as they ran back and forth across the wires, dodging the pellets being fired at them.

It wasn't until recently that I questioned Bobby, my older brother, about that incident, because I really didn't know the story behind the strange scene that I have carried in my memory all these years. He told me the following story.

One day while he and my brother George were watering their cattle, they happened to taste the water and found it to be bad. A climb to the top of that old forty-foot water tower and a "peek-see" confirmed their fears: dead rats were floating in the water. Contamination of that precious life source had begun, so it was decided to drain the water tower. They discovered hundreds more of these pesky creatures alive and in the process of running to the tower to drink and then running to the barn for food. Back and forth they went.

Pellet guns in hand, Bobby stood at the back of the house near the kitchen door while George settled down at the corner of the barn some forty yards away. And as the rats began to run to safety away from the empty water tower, the guns went pop! pop! pop!

I think of that incident as I read the story of the living water Jesus offered the Samaritan woman at the well. Perhaps you could say that she had spent a lot of years filling her bucket of life with "impure water." Not being careful to watch for things that would spoil her life source, her taste buds began to get accustomed to the tainted flavor, and a sickness took over her soul.

The story goes that Jesus came to town one day, sat down by her at the well, and offered her living water. She couldn't resist the temptation to accept His gift; and as she did, her life was restored and her soul made healthy again.

It is not so unlike the condition our livestock would have been in if my brothers had not come to their rescue, ridding the water tower of its contaminants and restoring within its circular boundary fresh and life-sustaining water.

"Everyone who drinks of this water shall thirst again; but whoever drinks of the water that I shall give him shall never thirst."
John 4:13–14

Alone

Into the quiet, the empty, I go,

The questions that never go away grow louder.

Yet

knowing,

I walk into the space which knows no bounds,

as if I'm drawn.

The aloneness!

Not real it seems.

I make it so

by ignoring

the presence of the One

who fills all void.

Merry doesn't ignore the presence of the One who fills all void! All it takes is a step through the front door of her home, and immediately you realize that you're in the presence of a wonderfully creative person. Hanging on the walls is the exquisite needlework that has been the product of her life alone. I've often told her how envious I am of her incredible giftedness. To be able to design and create beautiful tapestries or quilts or to knit or crochet sweaters as effortlessly as she seems to do is truly a gift. But the price Merry pays to do such beautiful work is the price of being homebound day after day, month after month, year after year.

It wasn't always this way with Merry. After graduation from college with a degree in art, she began sculpting in welded steel and clay. That's when the problem with her back began. Osteoporosis and osteoarthritis began to take their toll on her body and her ability to continue her work. As her spine began to collapse on itself, she experienced great pain and for awhile was unable to walk any distance at all.

"I remember how afraid I was at the thought of becoming incapacitated," she said to me, in reflection. "I got up my courage to begin to pray that beautiful prayer of abandonment of St. Ignatius of Loyola, because I knew that I had to surrender my fear. So for eight years, I prayed his words. Great peace began to unfold, and it became easier to give God permission to take away my financial and physical abilities.

"I lost the freedom to be able to leave the presence of God in order to pursue the distractions of my own will," she continued, "and once that happened, I began to see how my prayers to be in a closer relationship with Him were answered."

I believe that Merry walked into that boundless space, drawn by her willingness to surrender the known, and to embrace that which God planned for her. As we visited the other day, I said that she reminded me of the psalmist who asked of God, "Lead me to the rock that is higher than I. For Thou hast been a refuge for me, a tower of strength against the enemy" (Ps. 61:2–3).

She thought for a moment and then replied: "The rock that is higher is, for me, above the common, everyday distractions. It is the rock of the recognition and confession of my sins. That is the key that unlocks the door to the praise of God's unrelenting love."

The Prayer of Abandonment

*Take, O Lord, and receive my entire liberty, my memory, my
understanding, and my whole will. All that I am, all that I have,
Thou hast given me and I give it again to Thee to be disposed of
according to Thy good pleasure. Give me only Thy love and
Thy grace; with Thee I am rich enough,
nor do I ask for ought besides.*

St. Ignatius of Loyola[5]

The Duck Who Came in from the Cold

Step forward.

Cross the threshold.

Safety dwells within My

Kingdom of Love.

My shelter is sweet.

My shelter is warm.

My shelter is

now and forevermore.

Come!

I AM

the One who stands

by the opened door.

 grew up with many ducks, but by the time I was twelve we had just one big duck left. Although I didn't spend a great amount of time playing with him, I think he knew that he was valued and loved.

I remember the night a "blue norther" was blowing through Texas. Its bone-chilling wind caused the temperature to tumble, and my parents became concerned for the outside pets.

Knowing they needed shelter, Mother decided to bend the rules and let them in the house for the night. When she opened the front door, the dogs and cats were found huddled on the doorstep, and in they ran. After all were accounted for, my sister and I paraded them down the hallway, behind the pantry, and into the furnace room where it was warm and cozy.

As we started up the stairs for bed, we heard a strange noise coming from outside the front door. We stopped to listen for the sound. It came once again, and this time we recognized it. Mother opened the door and there, standing right in the middle of the doorway, was the duck!

I don't recall who was more startled, our family or the duck! As we stood there, hoping Mother would let him in, too, I remember wondering what he thought. I'm sure that he had watched all of the other creatures go in. I think he sensed that it was safe for him to venture in too.

Mother knew what she had to do, and as the door opened wider, the duck stepped across the threshold and into the hallway. With Mother leading the way, he waddled along behind her through the living room and into the guest bathroom where he spent that very cold winter night.

It doesn't matter who we are to God. The Scriptures remind us that God shows no partiality (Rom. 2:11). So if you're tired of trying to make it on your own, walk or run or even waddle to Him! Let Him lead you into the safe haven of His love. Snuggle up to Him just as a chick would nestle under the wings of the mother hen. He will give shelter and warmth down into the depths of your heart and soul.

Let me take refuge in the shelter of Thy wings.
Psalm 61:4

And there will be a shelter to give shade from the heat by day, and refuge and protection from the storm and the rain.
Isaiah 4:6

The Prayer That Heals

Let Me see through your eyes.

Let Me hear through your ears.

Let Me touch with your hands,

and walk with your feet.

Let Me be.

Let Me be.

Let Me be.

ME!

As she gently touched my forehead, Beth, my massage therapist, silently prayed as she began working her skilled hands and fingers in a manner that relieved me of a bad tension headache. I was finally freed from the pain that had lodged itself in my forehead, neck, and shoulders. It was a good time to remember that throughout the Gospel accounts, Jesus tells us to bring our needs to Him in prayer.

John 15:16 says, "You did not choose Me, but I chose you, and appointed you, that you should go and bear fruit, and that your fruit should remain, that whatever you ask of the Father in My name, He may give to you."

Things haven't changed for us today. Just as Jesus called His original band of followers, He calls us to become His disciples in our broken, sin-sick world. When we respond to the call, we become Eucharistic people—chosen, broken by our sin, but blessed in our brokenness and given out for the love of our fellowman. Living in this relationship to Jesus gives us the right to ask for the things that we need.

There is also the fine print I need to reread often. It is a command He gives to those who want to be inheritors of His kingdom. For John 15 also says that Jesus will abide in us if we abide in His love and keep His command to love others.

I vividly remember one spring night in the month of May when, after having looked at the famous painting of the annunciation to Mary by Fra Fillipo Lippi, I had gone to sleep with Mary's words on my lips: "Behold the handmaid of the Lord; be it unto me according to thy word" (Luke 1:38, KJV).

For one entire year I prayed that prayer, trusting that God would use me as He chose.

Sometimes I have found it hard to love others. It means that I have to invest my life in theirs, and that can be hard. I have discovered that when I'm asked to pray for their healing, however, I am fulfilling the command to love them.

For many years I have felt drawn into this ministry. When I pray for healing, I believe it occurs. Perhaps not always with visible results, but nevertheless effectively manifesting itself in the one for whom I have prayed.

I was recently visiting with a close friend and was reminded of the time when she was in the hospital for an abdominal blockage, and a surgical procedure was ordered for the following day. Hearing the anxiety in her voice when she called with this news, I went to visit her. I entered her room and stood at the foot of her bed. Gently touching her, I asked the Lord to remove the obstruction. Later that evening she phoned another close friend and asked for her prayers also. When the doctor examined her the next morning, he found no evidence of the blockage. She had been healed.

"Bitsy," she said, "I don't know if the healing was the result of your prayer or the prayers of others. All I know is that I was healed." It really didn't matter whose prayers were answered. What mattered most of all was that I loved her enough to go and to pray for her and she was healed.

Incredible things can happen when we pray! Once during a healing mission held at our church, I sat directly behind someone who had come forward for healing of a badly bruised knee. She had been struck by a car earlier that day. We were all asked to pray silently, sitting right where we were.

Afterward she told me that she began to feel a warmth coming from over her left shoulder. Since I had been sitting directly behind her, she felt that it was my prayer that had touched her most deeply. The bruises disappeared, and she was freed of pain.

On another occasion, I prayed throughout the day while another close friend underwent an operation. I prayed specifically that she would have no back pain when she came out from under the influence of the anesthesia. Having recently had a similar surgical procedure, I recalled the bad pain that I had experienced. Visiting her a few days later, I commented that I had hoped her back pain was not as severe as mine had been. She looked at me inquisitively and said, "What pain?" She had not experienced any.

I believe God wants us to be whole, for it has been noted that about 80 percent of Jesus' ministry while He was on earth was that of healing. It appears to me that He is doing the same today through the faithful prayers of His followers. I am sometimes blind to the healing that occurs, yet I know that I must pray because I believe that I am a handmaid of the Lord. God is the One who heals, but sometimes it is my hands, feet, voice, and heart He needs to do His work. His love and mercy do the rest.

> Now there are varieties of gifts, but the same Spirit.
> And there are varieties of ministries, and the same Lord.
> And there are varieties of effects, but the same God
> who works all things in all persons.
> But to each one is given the manifestation of the Spirit
> for the common good. For to one is given
> the word of wisdom through the Spirit,
> and to another the word of knowledge
> according to the same Spirit; to another faith
> by the same Spirit, and to another gifts of healing
> by the one Spirit, to another the effecting of miracles,
> and to another prophecy, and to another
> the distinguishing of spirits, to another various
> kinds of tongues, and to another the interpre-
> tation of tongues. But one and the same Spirit
> works all these things, distributing to each one
> individually just as He wills.
> 1 Corinthians 12:4–11

abiding
in His Mercy

The Diving Lesson

Gentle waters swirled,
yet my heart pounded.
I must descend.
I had to trust.

Fear grabbed.
I became a captive
kept
from the joy of going deep down,
down,
down
to view the wonder
of an unknown world.

I saw an outstretched hand.
Beautiful, strong hand
waiting.
Patiently waiting.
"Reach out, take hold," my pounding heart begged.
I reached.
And suddenly fear's broken chains fell.
Freedom came.

Still, printed in my mind,
a lasting picture of promise given.
My hand in His
brings peace.

 t was my idea that Rollins and I take scuba diving lessons. I thought it would be a sport that we could enjoy together. I didn't realize I would have a problem with fear. Certainly Rollins wouldn't; as a boy he had spearfished off the jetties of Port Aransas during long, hot summers on the Texas coast.

And so we took the "plunge." We sought out the best diving school in town and joined the next beginner's class. We liked our instructor, Rick, right away as we found him to be patient with our slow learning.

Before we ever got in the water, we were taught many things in the classroom, such as necessary swimming techniques, water currents and how to navigate them, the technique of buddy breathing, and much more. We took a written test at the end of the six-session classroom period, and we celebrated our passing grades.

With our confidence and anticipation high, we purchased our equipment. It was heavy and bulky and numerous: wet suits, booties, fins, buoyancy compensator vests, weight belts and weights, regulators, face masks, diving watches, gloves, and flashlights. We were told that our face masks had to fit snugly over our eyes and nose or they would fill with water and we could drown. Time was spent adjusting and readjusting them on our heads. The vest and regulator were awkward. I felt clumsy and restricted.

We quickly realized we were responsible for our equipment working properly because our very lives depended on it, and I did my best to pay attention to Rick as he went over all of the safety precautions.

Finally came our lessons in the water. At last, we were really going to begin to dive. I suddenly realized that I had to learn to be comfortable being dependent on an outside source for air. That's what the word *scuba* stands for—"self-contained underwater breathing apparatus."

We arrived at that first session and quickly changed into our suits. With all of my equipment in place, Rick strapped the heavy tank of air to my back. Suddenly, I began to wonder why I had ever thought I wanted to learn this sport. I began to hyperventilate. Am I having fun yet? I asked myself as I looked over at Rollins, who smiled back. It was apparent that he was!

The next few moments seemed like an eternity as I waited, teetering under the weight of my air tank, until I was given the signal to enter the water. I took the plunge, and fear seized me as I began to descend. Rick must have sensed it. Because as I hung there, trying to propel myself downward with the kick of my fins, suddenly I looked in front of me and saw his outstretched hand. Looking back over his shoulder, he motioned for me to take it. When I did, he gently led me into deeper water. My attention immediately shifted from my fear to his gentle lead.

I have found that there are many difficult lessons to learn in life. I've had to let go of the fear of going deeper into the heart of God. Instead I've learned that depending on Him for my life breath leads me into a whole new world. I've discovered it to be breathtakingly beautiful yet unattainable through my own strength.

God calls me to be a risk taker. Growing through the pain of low self-esteem, I have learned that I am capable of nurturing the gifts I was given in order to make my life count. Whether it be my attitude or my confidence and trust in myself or others, it becomes an awareness of the Truth. I don't want to go through life asleep. God wants me wide awake to live fully within each moment.

When I was baptized into the body of Christ, I became marked as Christ's own forever. I became His disciple. He didn't leave me to my own poor devices but endowed me with all I'll ever need to enter into whatever deep waters He may lead me. His hand is always there, ready to embrace mine. All I have to do is take it and trust that by His grace and mercy, He will lead.

Where can I go from Thy Spirit?
Or where can I flee from Thy presence?

If I ascend to heaven, Thou art there;
If I make my bed in Sheol, behold, Thou art there.
If I take the wings of the dawn,
If I dwell in the remotest part of the sea,
Even there Thy hand will lead me,
And Thy right hand will lay hold of me.
Psalm 139:7–10

The Vinedresser

Never aware of the dying
until
the Light reveals
its useless and misshapen form.
The branch
unfit
to remain attached
to that which was created
for fruitfulness.

He comes
and then it happens!
What once was alive now falls
lifeless
to the ground.
And new life seems to come quickly,
defining greater strength.
Maturing!
Grounded by its roots which lay deep within
the One
who formed the seed.

When I walked into Beth's room for the first time, the morning light flooded her bed revealing her misshapen form. I fought back the feeling of revulsion. Scleroderma had taken its toll! She was the first patient that I, as a hospice chaplain, had ever seen with this dreaded disease.

Scleroderma is a progressive disease that attacks the skin and internal organs with fibrous deposits of connective tissue.

Patients eventually lose the function of fingers and feet. There is pain, stiffness, and muscle weakness. Eventually, swallowing and breathing become impaired, and the patient takes on a mummy-like appearance as the skin is stretched extremely tight across the skeleton of the body.

A contorted smile and a disfigured hand reaching out to me defied the disease's ability to claim Beth's spirit! She had reached a level of maturity in the knowledge and love of the One who had created her and who had gifted her with the power to transform moment after moment of death-waiting into times of great joy for me. As the months rolled by and I continued to make weekly visits to her bedside, I clearly saw the truth born out of Jesus' promise to those who abide in Him.

Beth, the ex-wife of a famous sports figure, loved to tell me stories as she reflected on her life. I never heard her complain, except about visitors who wanted to get "too morbid" about her impending death. She just wanted to laugh as she thought back over the fun times she had knowing Jesus.

But in her final weeks, as the daily living began to drain her spirit, it became harder for me to make my visits. I had begun to feel depleted of my own energy and ability to be present to her and to the other patients I was seeing as well. In fact, I had become so drained that the last time I saw her, I was two days late for my appointed visit. When I finally arrived at her home, I was greeted at the door by her daughter, who looked at me with hurt and disappointment as she said, "Where have you been? Mom has been waiting to see you before she dies."

The time had come, finally! With a deep sense of sorrow, I leaned over her bed, gave her a smile, and kissed her on the forehead as I silently said my good-bye.

Her funeral was a celebration of the goodness of knowing Jesus Christ as her Lord and Savior. She requested that I give the homily and, in it, invite people to receive Him into their lives. The disease that cut away at her body had done its pruning well. What remained was the pure essence of a free spirit that had the power to transform the lives of others who came into her presence by pointing them to the Savior of the world.

Several weeks after Beth died, a framed, embroidered piece that had hung in her hallway was given to me by her daughter. I was deeply touched that Beth had wanted to leave me something of hers. As I held it in my hands, I realized that it said all that needed saying about God's gracious mercy and the healing in Beth's life. The inscription reads:

There is no box
made by God
nor us
but that the sides
can be flattened out
and the top blown off
to make a dance floor
on which to celebrate life.

"If you abide in Me, and My words abide in you, ask
whatever you wish, and it shall be done for you."
John 15:7

Starshine

O bright burning light,
magnificent stellar wonder!
You sought to show,
to give a clue,
where new life lay.
You, bright heavenly being,
were created by Him to be a guide,
trusted
by wise men from afar
and by more simple folk nearby,
who wondered at the meaning of your brightness.

I, too, was born to shine!
A creature sparked by radiant
Trinity,
to light a path,
to show the way
to love,
to life complete.

Yes!
That common bond between us has a purpose,
its grand design,
its beauty matched by none.
A tapestry of glory we've become!
All creatures and all creation to be
a light
for those who may not see,
or know
the One who gave us being.
The Christ!
The true and only source of light.

piphany! The star shone brightly, heralding the birth of Jesus and leading the three wise men to His dwelling place. It was a time of quiet celebration and great joy. Their long search for the King had come to an end (Matt. 2:1–11). The fulfillment of their dreams lay before them. Wonder matched their gratitude over the discovery of the babe.

These humble men of great wealth lay before the newborn King their gifts of gold, frankincense, and myrrh.

There was a time when our family traveled to the Rio Grande Valley of Texas so that a very close friend and I could celebrate our birthdays together. Although the drive was long, the trip was important. My friend had cancer, and no distance seemed too far to go as we knew the number of her days was decreasing.

Upon entering their home, instant laughter signaled the joyful reunion of our two families. We had chosen to stay close, bound by a common love of God and of one another. It would be impossible to put a value on those times we shared together. Death for her came after seven hard years. Although God didn't choose to cure her of the cancer, as I reflect on those happy birthday celebrations, I know the time we shared together was filled with healing.

I've sometimes wished that I could have lived in the time of Jesus' birth and, like the wise men, been able to present my gift to Jesus. What would I have given Him? Would I have been willing to give away a treasured possession? What value do I place on the gift of my love? I know that it costs more than good intentions. It costs time, sometimes money, and a lot of emotional energy. Yes, it is a precious gift to give another the gift of my love. In all honesty, I believe that is the gift I give to Christ, as well.

And about that star. I like to imagine there is one somewhere in that glorious stellar space above that shines brightly each time we wrap our love around the hearts of those we call our friends.

"This is My commandment, that you love one another,
just as I have loved you."
John 15:12

Cake in the Cabinet

Why did I hide it?
That which You so lovingly gave me.
Was it for hope of greater riches?
Or for pursuit of my own desire?
O, that I could have recognized the prize
I took and buried deep within.
To ignore. To deny.
Why?
Because it called me to be authentic.
To become the real and only self
You created me to be.
I wasn't ready.
I didn't trust.
I didn't know that only through that gift
would come true happiness
and wealth
beyond measure.

he discovery in the bathroom cabinet appeared to be treasure! I don't remember now what I went there to look for, but when I went into my brother's bathroom and opened the towel cabinet, way back behind a mountain of folded hand towels, there it was—a wedge of my godmother's delicious chocolate cake, which was our family's very favorite. I reached inside, eagerly pushing aside the towels to claim the prize. Much to my dismay, it was like a piece of concrete! Later I found out that it had been put there about a month earlier and obviously forgotten!

When it came to chocolate, my mother was a sneaky character. She would go to ridiculous extremes, it seemed to us children, to hide her addiction to it. On more than one occasion, we would chance upon piles of discarded chocolate candy wrappers. And once, I caught the dog licking an empty pan of chocolate sauce that mother had quickly shoved under her bed when she heard me approach her room.

So the discovery of the cake in the cabinet was just another one of her plots to hide a treasure from us so that later she could enjoy it all to herself! How sad to find it hard as rock! I was certainly out of luck, and so was Mother. It seemed that everyone lost out on that particular find that day.

I wonder what God thinks when He sees us hide the treasure He's given us so deep down inside ourselves that His gifts become like fossilized pieces of chocolate cake! I surprise myself when I am aware that I do this, usually because I lack faith in my own giftedness to make a difference for Christ's sake in someone else's life. I know that God desires me to use His gifts much more than I desire my godmother's chocolate cake, yet I believe our systems get addicted to the "sweets" of life, whatever form they take. We crave more and more, and can't imagine what it would be like to go without that which we think gives us nourishment. But what really feeds us are the untold treasures deep within ourselves that nourish others. For me, it is the knowledge of God's healing love for us.

"For to everyone who has shall more be given,
and he shall have an abundance;
but from the one who does not have,
even what he does have shall be taken away."
Matthew 25:29

Free Flight

I cling to the bar.
The rod familiar to my grasp,
is easy to hold, safe,
yet
the space ahead is void!

I hear from beyond
that Voice of calm assurance.
"Let go. Reach beyond!
Don't count the cost.
Trust!
I AM
strong arms which hold you
cradled as a child.
In faith, by grace
you can let go."

With open hands I stretch beyond.
He delivers me safely,
into new realms of love
which know no bounds.
Freedom!

 am learning that when I stretch out my open hand to God, let go of that familiar old "bar," and trust in His grace, the result is great freedom from burdens that have become unbearable. There is a reason for my change of mind. I used to let what I did in the name of "good deeds" become so consuming that I burned out. I am convinced this often happens to people who give themselves to volunteerism, whether it be at their local church or in their community. I now recognize that my need to control a situation or to please people sent my compulsive behaviors into overdrive! Unfortunately, we live in a world of compulsive behaviors that bump up against one another more frequently than we realize or care to admit.

In His own way, Christ modeled for all of us a life of healing service. We're not told that He healed everyone, only those to whom, for whatever reason, He was led. He knew because He spent time in prayer asking that His Father's will be done, then trusting that it was.

He told us that if we would live life His way, our load would not be burdensome. In fact, He said it would be easy! It has taken me many years to let "easy" be OK. I've sometimes experienced feelings of guilt over being blessed by prosperity and believing that I've not done enough for those less fortunate. I've often wondered, What is "enough," anyway?

Holding on to the safety bar of what I allow to become burdensome has often dammed up my God-given creative spirit. I'm learning that in order to live in freedom I must find the place where I fit. It has not been easy, but I know when I arrive there. For then I feel drawn to the task at hand, not driven.

I like the way Frederick Buechner describes this place in his book, *Wishful Thinking: A Theological ABC*: "The place God calls you to is the place where your deep gladness and the world's deep hunger meet."[6]

I recently read in the newspaper about Shamu, the killer whale who lives at Sea World. It seems that one afternoon during a performance, a small bird flew into the performing pool, became soaking wet, and couldn't fly out. The story goes that Shamu's trainers gave her the "fetch" sign, and off she swam, opening her huge jaws and closing them shut over the little bird. Then she swam back to her trainers and opened her mouth to reveal the little bird sitting on the tip of her tongue. One of the trainers lifted it out of her mouth and gently dried it off. With new-found freedom, it flew away. What a wonderful analogy of joint ministry in the name of love!

Christ calls me to go beyond myself and into unknown spaces—not alone, but sharing the load with others who call Him Lord. A healing freedom comes when we respond that way to His call.

> Living is to love him,
> Serving him to know his freedom.
> Come along with us to join the praise of Jesus.
> Come to Jesus now.
> Come to live his word rejoicing.[7]

"Take My yoke upon you, and learn from Me, for I am gentle and humble in heart; and you shall find rest for your souls. For My yoke is easy, and My load is light."
Matthew 11:29–30

Brotherly Love

Across endless miles and

through years of forever,

we'll keep constant

the step of love.

Hand in hand.

Heart to heart.

We'll love because

He first loved us.

n 1953, I graduated from a boarding school in Connecticut. My brother George was determined to be with me on that momentous occasion, so he hitchhiked from his Marine base in California clear across the country. Hitchhiking was something he had done frequently when he was a younger boy, but California to Connecticut was still a far piece! He had planned to fly on a military air transport plane from his base for most of the way; however, he had been "bumped" a short distance into the journey. So he resorted to the old familiar foot travel, hoping that friendly drivers would be kind and offer him rides to enable him to arrive at my school in time.

My parents arrived amid the farewells to friends. They were a welcome sight. I was not prepared, however, for the surprise that unfolded. That George would entertain the idea of attending my graduation never entered my mind. Therefore, his entrance into my dormitory room, dressed in full Marine uniform, caught me by great surprise and reduced me to tears. To this day I can feel the impact of seeing him standing there. I was overwhelmed by this demonstration of his love for me. This has continued to be a pattern throughout our lives as brother and sister. Through the years, he's continued to show up at the most unexpected and neediest of times.

Even though George and I were born into the same biological family, we view life through different eyes. I was the youngest child of four, the baby sister who, in many ways, was our father's pet. George was the second child and second son, who, like many "in the middle," often struggled to be himself. As siblings do, we have sometimes made mistakes in judging one another, and unkind words have been spoken, but they have always been forgiven.

George has always lived out his belief in the value and power of friendship as well. He keeps current with innumerable lifelong friends, no matter where they live. At times, he has gone to incredible lengths to be with them whenever he has sensed their need, just like he sensed mine on graduation day. In many different contexts throughout the Gospel accounts, Christ speaks of this kind of love which causes someone to go that extra mile—or two or three thousand—for the sake of another.

Love flourishes in those circumstances, and a healing power emanates from that kind of love force. To make the extra effort to be with someone or to give encouragement by word or deed does wonders for the human heart in more ways than we can know. Blessed am I to have had George in my life all of these years!

Be kindly affectioned one to another with brotherly love.
Romans 12:10, KJV

The Gift of Feeling

"Go forth," You say.
Yet, hesitations come.
Your invitation entices,
challenges.
I hear Your voice
and want to follow,
yet
am I really sure?

Yes!
It is Your call.
I've heard You speak before.
You have a way
of calling
those You've chosen.
They hear!
They know!

So one step forward
leads to another,
then another.
It seems more clear,
and then confirmed.
"Go forth," You say?
Yes! I will!
And joy will follow.

 n reading *Wisdom Distilled from the Daily*, I came across this statement: "'In hell,' the Vietnamese write, 'the people have chopsticks but they are three feet long so that they cannot reach their mouths. In Heaven, the chopsticks are the same length, but in Heaven the people feed one another.'"[8]

I put the book down and remembered my brother Bob, "Bobby" as I still call him. How well he, too, has demonstrated brotherly love through words of encouragement. In 1977 he was instrumental in seeing that I was named chairperson of the newly organized diocesan hunger committee. I worked at this position with intense interest, and with my leadership began a fifteen-year project we endearingly named "Operation Grapefruit."

It all began when a friend, a citrus grower in the Rio Grande Valley, desired to give away surplus grade A grapefruit. Weekly, between the months of November and April, he shipped two thousand boxes of fruit, each containing about twenty grapefruit, anywhere we asked—provided it reached the poor and infirm. For years, San Antonio received two truckloads weekly, while many other trucks were dispersed to other areas of need.

One particular winter morning, I followed a truck sent to El Paso with fruit to be distributed in the poverty-stricken area of Juarez, Mexico. I joined a small group of Episcopalians on a van that was driven across the border by a beloved Roman Catholic priest and his assistant, who worked at a food bank within Juarez's impoverished area. I never could have imagined what I saw that day. Old, discarded refrigerators sitting amid acres of smoking garbage had become homes for some. Others had made homes of cardboard boxes tightly clustered together along ditch-lined dirt roads.

Our van first stopped in front of a house where we had been told a young family with a very sick baby lived. Soberly, we climbed the tire-lined dirt hill to the entrance and were immediately welcomed inside by a tired young mother who held a small child in her arms. It took only one look to wrench my heart! The baby cried pitifully as gnats swarmed around its eyes, which were partially matted shut. I don't remember what was said, but the next thing I knew, I found myself joining the rest of our group in laying on hands upon the child's feverish forehead. With each word prayed, there appeared to come forth a tremendous force of energy. I could only describe it as the love of God. When I got back to the bottom of the little dirt hill, the pain I had just experienced was too much, and I sobbed.

We drove in silence to the food bank where we were to distribute the grapefruit. To my surprise, we were greeted by lots of happy people who had come from menial jobs to obtain food for their families. They possessed great dignity, which deserved my deepest respect. I felt honored and humbled being in their presence; and, as I handed out the fruit, I felt I was placing it into the hands of kings and queens!

I was overwhelmed by the powerful presence of the Holy Spirit as I watched and listened to these people gathered together, sharing stories of what God had done for them through the day and singing His praises. It became apparent to me that these simple people lived day by day, flooded by the mercy and miracles of a great and loving God. Jesus Christ was their only possession, and He was everything to them.

So what does all of this have to do with the gift of feeling? As I titled this writing, I glanced at my bookshelf to the spine of a lovely book with the same title by the renowned Swiss psychiatrist Paul Tournier. In it, he directs the reader's attention to the age-old need all humans have for subjectivity, emotions, tenderness, and interest in personal relationships—all of which are usually left to women to cultivate. Like many of my soul sisters, I struggle with a sensitivity that is at times too fragile. I lean into another's pain to the detriment of my own well-being. Prudence often cautions me to play it safe, but the unbelievable sights of Juarez came tumbling into my narrow and comfortable little world as a shattering revelation. The gift of feeling, of being concerned enough and maybe a little curious, too, caused me to venture into a wider space and see the reality beyond my own small world. I consider myself fortunate. By going out, being true to who I am, I began to experience a new health in my soul and an effective ministry for Christ.

The sick little child over whom we prayed was healed.

By faith Abraham . . . went out, not knowing where he was going.
Hebrews 11:8

Shouts of Joy

Hold me fast
to that Heart which gives life.
Its beat deep within gives
a rhythm
to live by,
to love by.

Hold me fast
in Your arms.
There is life-giving strength—
strength to sustain,
strength to send out
to others who need
Your love.

Hold me fast,
so that I may know
the pace of Your walk.
To follow each step
You take into those dens
of creative sorrow
and out into spaces
where dancing
and celebration live!

 few months after the trip to Juarez, Charles, a photographer friend who had also gone on that trip, accompanied me on a similar "grapefruit" mission. This time we traveled to Fort Defiance, Arizona, to the heart of the Navajo Indian reservation, where we found Native Americans living in impoverished conditions.

As the truckload of grapefruit was placed temporarily in the classroom of their small school, I was surprised to learn that these people didn't know what grapefruit was. It was foreign to their land, but they accepted the fruit graciously and named the yellow orbs "bitter oranges." Furthermore, several of their teachers made a nutritional study so that they could teach its benefits to their people. Finally, so as not to waste any part, after they ate the fruit, the skins were ground up and used as fertilizer for crops.

I was deeply touched by a wonderful elderly lady I met there. To this day I can close my eyes and remember her on that day so many years ago. Although she was legally blind, she lived alone in a tiny shack out from Fort Defiance. We made the trip by Jeep through deep snow into the back country. Arriving at her home, I slowly opened the door into her one-room dwelling and came face-to-face with her. As she stretched out her arm to take my hand, the expression of gentle radiance on her face spoke volumes. Her devotion to God and the joy she knew in her impoverished life tugged at my heart.

Impoverishment is regarded by some as a sought-after treasure from God. This gift was discovered by Ivan Illich who went in search of it by living in the Sahara Desert to be near the Franciscan order of Little Brothers founded by Charles de Foucauld. Here are his words in the forward of Carlo Carretto's book, *Letters from the Desert:* "The emptiness of the desert makes it possible to learn the almost impossible: the joyful acceptance of our uselessness."[9]

The memory of that remarkable lady was the gift I received in exchange for the box of fruit we brought to her. In fact, it continues to heal and enrich my spirit, for I have come to realize that it is good when I am embraced by poverty. It sends me to my knees where I need to be more often. That is when my sin of pride is replaced by the gift of humility.

O glorious Triune God-Father, Son, and Holy Spirit—may we call Your name blessed forever! Help us to want only Your fullness, so that we, too, can be light where there is darkness, and joy where there is sorrow!

For you will go out with joy,
And be led forth with peace;
The mountains and the hills will break forth into
shouts of joy before you,
And all the trees of the field will
clap their hands.
Isaiah 55:12

Worship

Those simple acts of adoration,

what do they mean to You?

A bend of knee

at the foot of Your cross.

A gesture

made by upraised hands.

The song of souls adoring,

lifted to heights unknown.

What does it do for You,

O Holy One

who calls us "friends"?

We do it awkwardly.

Yet You smile

at the small gestures

born in the hearts of those

who choose Your way.

 sat in church one Sunday and in the middle of singing a glorious praise song, I watched a friend struggle with grief. She began to cry uncontrollably. The singing of that lovely song had obviously provoked some emotion that caused the tears to flow. Another friend came and sat next to her and embraced her. I knew what had caused the grief. Fresh memories of the tragic accident that took the life of her six-year-old daughter flooded my mind. I sat there wondering what it must have been like for her and her husband during that long, agonizing night of waiting while the life of their little girl slipped farther and farther away with each passing minute. Silently, I began to weep too.

Sometimes we come together in a dutiful manner to worship the Lord on Sunday. In my church, all is very much in order. We sing, and we pray, and we do our worship well. We come as individuals, each from our own homes, and with our own joys and sorrows. But when we enter the door of that sanctuary, we become one body, Christ's body! When one member suffers, we all suffer. That's what a body is all about.

God desires to have us worship Him. There's power in the praise; for when we praise, our hearts are opened to the touch of the Divine Physician who reaches deep down inside and binds up our wounds and heals our scars. That healing is aided by those who worship with us, who become the comforting arms and soothing touch of Christ.

To the One on the Throne! To the Lamb!
The blessing, the honor, the glory, the strength,
For age after age after age.
Revelation 5:13, *The Message*

A Mother's Pain

Radiating deep inside

a sweet, sweet gleam of life

flowed

from the Father's deepest

well of joy.

And buried within one tiny cell

began to grow my own peculiar

suffering.

From that first moment

O cherished love,

until my breath is stilled

I must claim

a mother's pain.

For it is my Father's will.

 recall the June afternoon my husband drove me to the hospital to give birth to our first child, our precious Ann. I cannot remember too well what I was feeling other than the intermittent contractions. Rollins had carefully tucked me into the car for the twenty-minute ride. A few short hours later she was born. But motherhood didn't begin on that lovely June day. It began at the moment of her conception; and although she was conceived in an act of loving intimacy, the pain of motherhood took seed.

This unique pain often manifests itself in those early weeks and months of pregnancy with nausea, sleepiness, and other forms of discomfort. And the act of childbirth itself is painful. But can the hardship of the physical pain compare to the emotional suffering that is certain to follow as the child grows toward maturity and beyond?

My thoughts are with Mary, the mother of Jesus, and her words recorded in Luke's Gospel as she responded to Gabriel's incredible proclamation. Place yourself in her shoes. Can you imagine an experience of union with the Holy Spirit? Was it anything like our human experience? Could she know what was to be her special joy and agony as she walked through life with her son, our Savior? How horrible must have been her pain as she stood at the foot of the cross where He hung naked until He died! With absolute trust, she gave herself to God the Father when she became the Christ-bearer. Such faith in His will at her young age is almost beyond comprehension. Her love for Him must have been so pure.

Our children have brought us great joy, but their pain has been mine as well. Disillusionments have brought death to many of their hopes and dreams and, as a mother, I find myself standing by those crucifixion moments wanting to shield them from their own particular agony. I am so willing to suffer in order to spare them, but my own life experiences have taught me that going through pain brings healing and new growth.

Standing beside Mary at the foot of Christ's cross was His beloved disciple John, and it was into his care that Christ placed His mother for love and safekeeping the rest of her life. I feel sure that healing came through the comfort of John's strong arms as she rested in his embrace.

As a parent I am consoled by the knowledge that Christ does not abandon me in this task any more than He abandoned His mother. He promised that He would be with me always, even to the end of the age (Matt. 28:20). And I, too, am healed by the embracing love of others who walk with me along the way.

Behold the handmaid of the Lord;
be it unto me according to thy word.
Luke 1:38, KJV

Don't Talk with Your Mouth Full

Convicted,
I am found wanting!
The sin cuts off,
unravels the lifeline.
The tension,
broken.

Convicted,
I stand naked,
exposed, ashamed.
I rationalize, I think,
False guilt?
No. Real!
Committed so quickly.

I had no thought
that what I'd say
would hurt,
destroy, tear down
that friend who
seeks to walk with You.

I mused
and said once more
"I had no thought!"
O God! My sin exposed,
I am
convicted.

Not too long ago, I saw my big, yellow Labrador Retriever standing at the kitchen door whining to go out so that he could chase one of the neighborhood cats who frequents our backyard. He was so eager to bark and chase her that he almost knocked the screen door down to get out. When his paws hit the deck, he stopped. He couldn't bark, but he didn't know why.

"You can't bark with a bone in your mouth, silly dog," I hollered. It took him a moment before he realized he had to drop the bone if he wanted to sound like a fierce protector of his domain.

How many of us heard similar words from our parents when we were growing up, such as, "Don't talk with your mouth full of food." That's good advice for more reasons than one. It's hard to understand someone who speaks with his mouth full, and sometimes it's embarrassing.

When I was a hospice chaplain I was asked to visit Harold, who was dying of cancer. His whole family had made a commitment to follow Christ—that is, everyone except Harold. They were a Baptist family who were naturally grieved that their husband and father wasn't saved.

I remember the first morning I went to see him. His wife opened the front door and immediately began tearfully imploring me to do something or say something that might lead Harold to Christ. I quickly realized that my invitation to visit was hers, not his, and yet he consented to my coming.

I walked into his bedroom eager to get to know this man. For almost an hour I listened to his hunting and fishing stories. He smiled as he showed me his photos and the articles he had written for the newspapers about these happy experiences. He loved the outdoor life, and he loved telling me about it.

After awhile, he began to tire and lay quietly in bed. I spoke softly to him. "Harold, how are you spiritually?" He turned his face away from me, and I noticed a tear slide down his right cheek.

"I'm not anywhere," he said. "I never have accepted Jesus Christ as my Savior. I don't know why, either. All of my family have. I am the only one. I just never have."

A heavy silence fell upon the room. Then tumbling from my lips came these words: "Well, I know that Jesus loves you very much, Harold. And if you get curious, you may want to read the fourteenth chapter of the Gospel of John."

He lay there in silence. I told him good-bye and left the room. His wife took me to the front door, still crying. Maybe I had let her down, yet I knew that I had done what I was to do.

I left town for a week, and when I returned to the hospice office, Harold's nurse greeted me. "Guess what happened to Harold," she urged, breathlessly. "I don't know. What happened?" I responded. "He accepted Jesus Christ as his Savior because of what you said to him."

Tearfully, I thought back on my final words to Harold. "I don't think it was what I said, but what I didn't say," I quietly responded. "You see, I didn't preach the Word to him, but just led him to it. And in the silence of the moment, he was nourished and transformed." It is for certain that spiritual healing had come to Harold through the Word of God.

So what does all of this have to do with speaking with your mouth full? It was St. Francis who said, "Preach Christ everywhere. Use words if necessary."

As a Christian, I need to feed on the Word of God, and then in the moment of quiet, let Him reveal to me the meaning of His will.

But no one can tame the tongue; it is a restless evil and full of deadly poison. With it we bless our Lord and Father; and with it we curse men, who have been made in the likeness of God.
James 3:8–9

Rendering unto Caesar

The voice within—gentle and strong!
Sometimes I protest to what I hear it say,
and turn from its truth.
Consistent, unchanging, it cuts into my soul
as if it were a sword
whose blade goes deep
into my sin of selfishness.

Its ring of truth will
haunt.
Discomfort turns to anguish.
War erupts.
A battle within!
Life threatened!
My mind shuts down to truth.

Now
Another's voice within,
so sweet and flattering!
Words softly spoken.
Chosen well to soothe
and comfort my sin-sick soul.
Yet, 'til my ear is tuned
to the lie exposed,
the enemy sneers triumphantly.

Once more
I turn my heart
to the One
whose voice is gentle, strong, and clear.
He calls me
to consider the consequences.
The choice
is always mine.

ometimes it happens—the Lord speaks to me clearly!
This particular morning was one instance. I finished
my morning prayers, walked out the front door for my

early morning jog, feeling so-o-o good! A whole day's activities lay ahead. Stepping lightly into the street I thought, *Lord, speak to me in ways I understand.* Immediately the familiar voice came into my mind: "Render unto Caesar the things that are Caesar's and to God the things that are God's."

I was surprised! What was that all about? I thought. I had not read that particular passage of Scripture for a long time, and I was puzzled that it came into my mind out of nowhere.

What do you mean by that? I countered.

"The Lord wants of you a repentant spirit," was the quick reply.

A convicting silence followed, one that did not leave me questioning too long. Because as the voice spoke those words, I was provided with some particulars—those things of which I needed to repent. As I continued to jog, I became aware of the people I had to speak with and the things I had to say. Risking pride, I knew what had to be said, and to whom—my family.

Funny thing! I didn't become anxious or defensive. And as I jogged toward home, my pace quickened and my steps grew lighter with expectation of what was soon to become, not an ordeal, but a blessing!

When I walked through the front door, down the hallway, and into the bedroom, I saw Rollins in the bathroom with shaving cream all over his face. Eager to get on with the task at hand, I blurted out, "Honey, I need to speak to you." Whenever I say something like that at inappropriate times, it has an unsettling effect on him! With very big, questioning eyes he cautiously asked, "What is it?"

"Not now," I said. "At the breakfast table."

He continued to look anxious. I assured myself that I calmed his fear with a smile before I walked into the kitchen to prepare breakfast.

Once seated at the table and after grace was said, I said to him, "I would like you to forgive me for all of the ways I have not honored you as my husband."

We had been married thirty-three years at that time. There were plenty of ways that I had not honored him. I knew that. So did he, because after a respectable pause he answered, "Oh, Bitsy, I always have."

I was surprised! He could have asked me what I meant. But both he and I knew that wouldn't have been honest. With gentleness he unveiled the truth, demonstrating the quality of love so necessary for a relationship to remain whole—forgiveness.

No more words seemed needed. A loving smile was shared, and the usual hurried good-bye kiss at the door was filled with fresh awareness of the power that love has when it is born out of obedience to God.

Visits with other members of my family followed. Each time I asked for forgiveness, it was quickly given. Some asked for mine in return. What a sense of wonder and peace and love all wrapped up into one big swelling of the heart!

Someone once defined the kingdom of God as the kingdom of right relationships. It certainly rang true for me that day!

Why it is so difficult to let go of that which causes His kingdom to be torn asunder with unresolved issues that not only tear at our hearts, but His as well. Healing comes to the forgiving heart!

*"Render to Caesar the things that are Caesar's; and
to God the things that are God's."*
Matthew 22:21

Pulling Chains

To return

dishonor

comes easy when

Christ is forgotten

and

I reflect upon my own

desires.

I become no better

than the soul

who knows Him not.

 o you allow people to "pull your chain" and "push your buttons"? When someone pulls my chain or "gets my goat," I give them power to produce in me a negative reaction that sends me reeling into my inner self to nurse my bruised and battered ego.

Not long ago my friend Ilene came over to take a walk with me. As we broke into a comfortable stride, she began to tell me

82

of an incident that had just happened to her that made her annoyed with herself and angry at another person as well.

She had gone into the drugstore to pick up a prescription she had ordered earlier by phone. She could see it sitting on the counter, already packaged, charged to her account, ready for her to pick up. But the salesclerk was unwilling just to hand it to her. Instead she made Ilene stand in line while she waited on several other people in front of her.

In Ilene's growing irritation, she began to sense that the girl was taking delight in making her wait.

"I found myself getting angrier as each minute passed," she told me, "and by the time she finally waited on me, I had become just as unpleasant to her as she had been to me. I really let her pull my chain, and I just hate it when that happens."

In the Beatitudes, Jesus said that the meek will inherit the earth. I heard one Christian expositor of the gospel define meekness as "the power to control power." When I think about that as a follower of Christ, I realize that the gift of the Holy Spirit is to enable me to live out my life victoriously among all the chain pullers in the world!

Yes, people do pull my chain, and I sometimes think they want to see me squirm! Next time I hope that they'll be disappointed.

For God has not given us a spirit of timidity
but of power and love and discipline. . . . And the Lord's bond-
servant must not be quarrelsome, but be kind to all,
able to teach, patient when wronged.
2 Timothy 1:7; 2:24

Sweet Chariot

Chariots don't have to have wheels
pulled by great maned stallions
all flashed out in colored plumes
racing through rising dust of sands.
Chariots may have oars instead
which row them bravely
through high seas
and into battlefields of mercy.

But chariots are driven
by those of intention
with missions to proclaim.
Perhaps angels
may even occupy the seat
when God takes command.

O, 'tis a gift to see
beyond appearances.
What meets the eye
may belie
all that there really is.
It is what's found within
that reveals the goodness
of our Lord.

he little boat that came motoring around the bend was a welcome sight to four weary fishermen. I still believe it was occupied by two angels who appeared as a man and his little boy. They came from out of nowhere that very cold and windy March day and rescued our family after we had been marooned for five hours on a long strip of land across

St. Charles Bay. They arrived only moments after we had gathered in prayer asking God to send us help, and just before Rollins and son-in-law Tim were to swim through the cold waters of the channel to the boat basin on the other side. The man and his son came with great speed and with big, broad smiles. Without a question asked, they quickly helped us into their small, bright turquoise wooden boat and took us to safety. They also disappeared as mysteriously as they appeared and were nowhere to be found later when we went in search of them with a carton of freshly cooked barbecue as a thank-you offering.

The morning had begun a little colder than usual. A "blue norther" was putting a chill on that early spring day, and the wind was blowing strong. However, it didn't seem bad enough to be dangerous for us to be out on the water. St. Charles Bay is one of our favorite bays along that strip of the Texas Gulf Coast, but it has never been very popular with other fishermen because the fishing is not generally good. So it didn't surprise us that we saw only an occasional crabber on the water that morning. They were so intent on working their traps that they never looked up to see our white handkerchiefs waving atop our fishing poles as distress signals while the cold north winds increased. Our little boat had traveled the length of the bay, all the way to the tip end, when it decided to give out on us.

We weren't too concerned at first. Some boat would travel up our way and spot us, we thought. Since we were in shallow water, we just stepped out of the boat onto the marshy shoreline and began the long trek back along St. Joe Island, singing and pulling the boat behind us. One hour, two hours, three hours went by. It was growing colder, and we began to think that our chances of seeing any other boats were getting slimmer with each passing minute.

What had initially begun as "high adventure" began to get tiring and annoying. Five hours had passed, and we had finally arrived directly across the channel from the boat basin where we had launched earlier that morning. We were tired, but Rollins knew that the only thing left to do was to swim the half-mile across the channel and find help. Since channels run deep, I began to get concerned, so I was glad to hear Tim announce that he was planning to join Rollins in the swim.

As they prepared to leave our daughter Ann and me on the shoreline, I hollered, "Let's pray before you try to swim that channel!"

Since I'm always feeling the need to pray, Rollins, who had gone ahead, remained standing where he was. So Ann, Tim, and I held hands. I prayed, "Lord Jesus, please send someone to help us."

Tim turned and began to walk out to join Rollins in the swim. Just as they were stepping into the channel, the little boat came around the bend.

We couldn't believe our eyes! Once we were on board, all huddled on the floor, we just sat there grinning at each other. Tim looked at me and over the roar of the motor, he said loudly, "He heard us!"

It was then that I said to the man driving the boat, "You're angels, aren't you?" His smile was his only response. He hardly spoke a word except to tell us that his name was Duane.

As we bid him and his son good-bye, we asked where they were staying. Duane told us they were camping at Goose Island State Park. We didn't think that we would have a hard time finding them. However, a drive through the small park didn't reveal a trace of them, nor were they still out on the water. We questioned folks around, but no one had seen a man and a little boy and a turquoise wooden boat!

As the Scripture story reads in 2 Kings, Elisha was wishing hard that his servant could see God's mighty angels poised for battle against their enemies. Sometimes that is my wish too. This day, I believe God granted me that wish. Of course, Duane's boat was not a "chariot of fire," nor were there enemies all around us, even though we were surely in some danger. But to this day, I believe God answered our prayer by sending angels to help us.

If we could only have the eyes to see God's angels at work every day in our lives, maybe we would truly believe the length, depth, and breadth of His love for us.

"O LORD, I pray, open his eyes that he may see." . . . And behold, the mountain was full of horses and chariots of fire.
2 Kings 6:17

Living Waters

Rivers flow with force unseen.
Sometimes quietly, gently
over rock and blade.
Sometimes gushing forth
with unimagined speed,
spilling into deep pools of calm.

My path becomes veiled.
I grope and stop, frozen by unknowing.
I fear to step again.
And in the void, I ask:
Where am I going?

But He who has created man and river
directs and purposes my path.
He who calls me to live abidingly
gives peace!
Faith
in this brings
Hope
in what lies ahead, unseen.
Love!

 have boated in rivers and have come upon waters rushing suddenly into a pool of utter calm. Once the water has been deposited there, it seems to go nowhere. The force of its current has been stilled, and its rush to go downstream has been temporarily detoured. I see that as an accurate way of describing my spiritual life as well.

It used to be that I couldn't have a prayer time without the Spirit of the Lord speaking clearly through the study of His Word. Now, oftentimes it moves into a different realm. It is not because I have closed my mind to His Word, but instead I have realized that I trust Him more with the silence. And with that deeper trust, I'm able to more clearly recognize His nudges and urgings on my life.

If I am to model my life after Christ and try to cooperate with His Holy Spirit who lives within me, then I must shut out the world more. Thomas Merton explains this position by saying: "We do not go into the desert to escape people but to learn how to find them; we do not leave them in order to have nothing more to do with them, but to find out the way to do them the most good. But this is only a secondary end. The one end that includes all others is the love of God."[10]

Right after my conversion experience some twenty-five years ago, the "story line" of life clipped right along as if I knew the plot before the play was ever written. I thought I knew God's rules for the game of life, for it was spelled out for me in black and white. Silly, arrogant me! The truth I uncovered was that life is rarely black and white. There is a lot of gray, and it seems to appear in our lives when we least expect or want it.

I can understand what St. John of the Cross meant when he described the dark night of the soul. I recognize the space he described, and I find consolation in the knowledge that it is a common place to be when one desires earnestly to make one's way step by step through God's kingdom. The silence and the darkness are much a part of the journey—a journey on which I believe God beckons those who choose to follow Him.

It is only the Living Water flowing from His abundant love that quenches my thirst on my journey. I find comfort and a kindred spirit in Thomas Merton's words as he continues to explain:

The only way to find solitude is by hunger and thirst and sorrow and poverty and desire, and the man who has found solitude is empty, as if he had been emptied by death. He has advanced beyond all horizons. There are no directions left in which he can travel. This is a country whose center is everywhere and whose circumference is nowhere. You do not find it by traveling but by standing still.

Yet it is in this loneliness that the deepest activities begin. It is here that you discover act without motion, labor that is profound repose, vision in obscurity, and, beyond all desire, a fulfillment whose limits extend to infinity.[11]

I don't know what will be except that it simply will be. As King Solomon wisely said, "Trust in the LORD with all your heart, / And do not lean on your own understanding. In all your ways acknowledge Him, / And He will make your paths straight" (Prov. 3:5–6).

Trust is the oar that eventually pushes me out of the still pools in my life. For I cannot stay out of the mainstream forever. Even though in the calm, still waters He gives peace and wisdom in a way that the world cannot give, acts of loving service must follow the times of stillness.

No, I do not know where I am going in His story, or how it will unfold, only that it will. And if I allow it, God's grace and perfect timing will carry me back into the flow of life to touch and heal the ones He brings along my way.

Faithful is He who calls you, and He also will bring it to pass.
1 Thessalonians 5:24

Lifeline

Tied as I choose to be.
Connected, supported, it holds firm,
but gives
so that I can move
at will through life.
MY CHOICE ALWAYS.
Freedom given?
Yes!
But only so far
will I go.

I stretch the line.
It twists, I turn,
and sometimes it strains
at my pull to be me,
untethered.
Yet it holds firm
and brings me back,
always to where I have to be.
The only place of survival,
is in the shadow of the cross.

he cross has always been a cherished symbol of my faith. However I had often found myself turned away by the crucifixes depicting the dying Christ until I recently visited with a Roman Catholic friend. He is the program coordinator of a retreat center, and the day I visited him there he was eager to show me the crucifix hanging in the chapel. As we approached the altar, my eyes fixed upon what I believe is one of the most agonizing Christ figures I have ever seen.

"Bitsy," Andy said softly, "it wasn't until I saw that crucifix that I realized the extent of the sacrifice Jesus Christ made on my behalf. There is something about His eyes that reflects such a deep sense of love. When I first looked up at His body with His forehead bloodied by the crown of thorns, His side pierced deeply by the sword, and His knees bent in tension and pain, all I could say was, 'How can You still look at me and love me?'"

We stood there for a moment in silence. Then Andy continued, "I have watched grown men who have come on retreat stand before that cross and weep as they have looked up at Christ. The awareness of the sacrifice He made on their behalf has brought reconciliation and conversion."

It's true that Christ's life didn't end that day on Calvary. He was resurrected on that first Easter Sunday almost two thousand years ago and ever since has been calling His followers to serve Him—Christ the risen King. Yet now I find I cannot serve Him truly if I have not embraced my own cross whose "beams" are comprised of all my past sins and failures. It is my own cross that keeps me tethered to His. As hard as I may try, I know that I will not become whole any other way.

My friend Andy was right. Sometimes I have to be confronted visually by the agony of Christ on the cross to remember that my sins put Him there. The good news is that His love for me overcame His death—and mine as well.

"Whoever does not carry his own cross and come after Me cannot be My disciple."
Luke 14:27

The Fast

My child, surrender
your self-centered ways.
A life-style not focused on
My will
deals a death blow to your soul.

Reach down deep.
Deep down
into the depths
of
your stored-up love.
Give
the only food
needed for the soul.

Don't hold back.
My love is needed everywhere.
Without it, people grow weak,
frail, and fade away.
Death
comes quickly
to the soul denied
My love.

Yes!
It will cost you.
More than you think you have
to give.
But remember My promise . . .
I will provide
what you need and so much more.

Watch,
see,
and know
that
I AM GOD ALMIGHTY!

 few years ago I had a conversation with my young friend Alexis about fasting. I was telling her how difficult it was for me to give up eating for even a short period of time. She laughed quietly and said, "Bitsy, I don't believe you can fast on your own. It has to be something that God calls you to do."

I could not argue with her. She had just recently completed a week's fast under the supervision of a Christian medical doctor. Her intent, however, was not to lose weight, as mine so often has been, but rather to deepen her relationship with Jesus Christ.

Shortly after our conversation, the practice of fasting began to open up a new world of living for her. Having become aware of a growing hunger deep within her spirit and realizing how desperate she was to break out of the empty life she was living, she realized she was starving for the real food that would put energy and life back into her spirit. She accepted a position with the International Foundation in Washington, D.C., a Christian ministry to the people who work on Capitol Hill. She resigned her job in San Antonio and began to seek funding for her own salary from family, friends, and her church.

Her work in Washington opened up many new vistas. Through the Servant Leadership School at the Church of Our Savior, taught by its pastor, Gordon Cosby, she learned how to lose her life in order to find it by serving others (Matt. 10:39).

By apparently divine circumstances, a year later she was invited by the wife of the president of Uganda to come work in Kampala. It was there, among the poorest of the poor, that she lost her heart to the Ugandan people and found the life she had been searching for.

She recently recalled for me an experience in which she felt overwhelmed by the reality of God's presence. On a road trip to Jinja with other Ugandan Christian women to hear their first lady speak, Alexis was the only white woman among a van full of blacks all speaking their native tongue. As she looked out over the expanse of the tea plantations, she became aware of how out of place she seemed to be. She told me that as the wind blew through her hair, it was as if the Holy Spirit was breathing into her, and she recalled the words of Paul when he said that there was nothing that could separate us from the love of God (Rom. 8:38).

In defining that experience she said, "Part of the mystery of God is that only when we empty our cup can God fill it. It's such a paradox to the meaning of what the world calls 'life.'"

Shortly afterward, she began work with an orphanage that is home for over seven hundred children, most of whose parents have died of AIDS. As she cared for those among them who were also dying, treating and carrying their failing, bleeding, foul-smelling bodies, she realized she had finally left her self-centered ways.

Her work with these beloved Ugandan friends continues. In the year and a half since she began at the orphanage, she has been instrumental in establishing a foundation in the United States whose goal it is to provide financial support for these children.

Alexis has been able to tap into the power of the fast that the prophet Isaiah describes. He does not challenge our gluttonous food habits so much as our self-centered lifestyles. It is a much harder fast to embrace unless, like Alexis, one intentionally draws close to the Lord and leans heavily on His power.

When I asked her to describe what happens when she fasts, she responded, "I find that I confront my emotions, including my anger toward God. I embrace them, and then I let them go, only to repeat that process over and over again. But what comes out of the fast is a clearing of the mind. All of the cobwebs are erased, and I realize I really can move from being self-centered to God-centered."

That is Alexis' story. It is not my story nor yours. Few of us are called by God to go to Africa. But I believe that as Christians we are called to a fast that will take us out of our own little worlds and into the worlds of others around us. Healing of the spirit comes mightily as we move outside of ourselves.

"*Is this not the fast which I choose, . . .*
to let the oppressed go free. . . .
And if you give yourself to the hungry,
And satisfy the desire of the afflicted,
Then your light will rise in darkness,
And your gloom will become like midday.
And the LORD *will continually guide you.*"
Isaiah 58:6, 10–11

Walking to the Music

Listen!
My voice like bells makes freedom ring.
Walk
gently through foreign lands.
Lost souls once seen as infidels
belong to My Father, too.

Their vision blurred.
Their eyes scarred.
They need to hear the music
of My love.
They yearn
to link their hands in yours.

Please!
For their sake,
listen to My children.
Don't just talk the talk.
Walk, child of the Light.
Walk the walk of Love.

 miss my friend Cathy. She has taught me so much about the healing power of God's Word as written in the Scriptures. She returned to Istanbul last week where she works with Youth With A Mission (YWAM). She has worked with YWAM for the last five years after having felt called to leave her seventeen-year teaching career. When she resigned her position at the middle school, she had just received the honor of being named the most outstanding teacher of the year in Austin, Texas.

She heard a call from God, however, so she packed her love for God alongside her gift of teaching and moved to Lausanne, Switzerland, the location of a YWAM training center. Her mission field became like a kaleidoscopic dance through Europe as she began to train young people of all nations in the art of discipleship so they can carry the good news of Jesus and His saving grace to people who do not know Him.

Currently, Cathy and these young emissaries are participating in the Reconciliation Walk, an exciting and challenging walk along the routes of the ancient Crusades that took place over nine hundred years ago.

From history books we know that these bloody rampages done in the name of Jesus Christ were the last time that the Church sent representatives to the Middle East in any large numbers. The outcome of these "missions" left a bitter trail that betrayed the true witness of the One who is called the Son of God.

Aware that evangelism for the sake of Christ is not possible until reconciliation is achieved, these young people carry with them a statement of apology written in Turkish and all other local languages to all Muslims, Jews, and even Greek Orthodox Christians for the way our Christian forefathers misrepresented the gospel of Christ during the Crusades.

"The Walk is the power of the gospel come alive," Cathy exclaimed as we sat together for our last visit before she left. "Sin separates us from each other and destroys all relationship, but when we meet at the Cross for forgiveness, we realize how great an impact God has on our lives. Being reconciled with one another brings healing, which gives birth to freedom and joy. Then and only then can God have the room to pour His love through us, and it is His lovingkindness that wins us all.

"Bitsy, I have spoken to many Turks who want to believe that we are supposed to be different. Some know of Jesus from reading the Scriptures, and they find it difficult to see Him other than a man of love and compassion. We know we have to walk these ancient routes in order for the prophecy of Isaiah to ring true."

When Cathy and I prayed together before she embarked on her mission five years ago, I asked the Lord to give me a special word for her. What came to my mind were words from a very old English nursery rhyme I hadn't thought of since my childhood. I was amused because it certainly wasn't what I had expected the Lord to reply, but nevertheless I was eager to share with her what I had heard.

"Cathy," I said, "the Lord gave me these words for you:

> Rings on her fingers,
> and bells on her toes.
> She shall have music
> wherever she goes."

Surprised, she looked at me for a moment through her big, brown eyes and then, tossing her head back in joyful laughter, she said, "Oh, how I know I will need to hear the music."

Now when Cathy comes to mind, I pray for the music to accompany her. She's told me that it has, for she has found that it would be impossible to walk the walk of Christ with a heavy heart. The melodious sounds of God's words of loving mercy have illumined her path and kept her steps light.

> *And it shall be said,*
> *"Build up, build up, prepare the way,*
> *Remove every obstacle out of the way of My people."*
> *For thus says the high and exalted One*
> *Who lives forever, whose name is Holy,*
> *"I dwell on a high and holy place,*
> *And also with the contrite and lowly of spirit*
> *In order to revive the spirit of the lowly*
> *And to revive the heart of the contrite. . . .*

Peace, peace to him who is far and to him who is near,"
Says the LORD, "and I will heal him."
Isaiah 57:14–15, 19

Now all these things are from God, who reconciled us to Himself
through Christ, and gave us the ministry of reconciliation, namely,
that God was in Christ reconciling the world to Himself,
not counting their trespasses against them,
and He has committed to us the word of reconciliation.
2 Corinthians 5:18–19

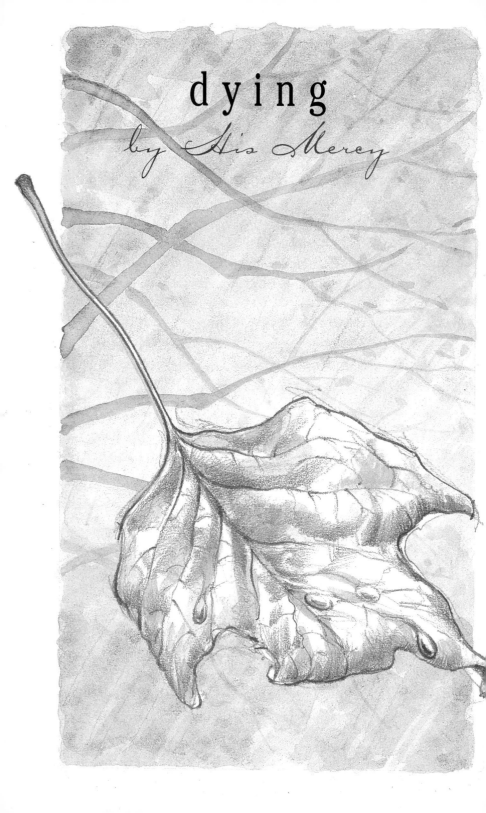

dying
by His Mercy

Trampled and Broken

"Who is my neighbor?"
That ancient voice asks.
Do I really want to know?
To be bothered, distracted,
from my own purpose and plans for glory and pleasure.
Dare I risk to go to those whose need I might fill?
To heal a trampled spirit, a broken heart.
To nurture with compassion and mercy.
The same which has been given me by some other life traveler
as I lay bruised along the roadside.

The question is answered in the asking!
The Christ in you, and you, and even
YOU
brought me to life.
Born from your poverty,
you sought to share the balm with me.
So I must, too!
I have no choice.
My health depends upon my sharing
or I'll be found again,
lying on the roadside of life.

 t seemed like my whole family lay scattered by the side of the road when my sister and brother-in-law were killed in a plane accident. Still in their twenties, they left behind three little girls, ages six, four, and fifteen months.

Their deaths and the grief that followed seemed unbearable. I can't imagine what my mother and father must have felt. A lot of decisions had to be made. Some might not have been wise, but when you're dealing out of grief, you do the best you can.

When the accident happened, the little girls were staying at the home of their baby-sitter. The awful task of having to pick them up and tell them of their parents' deaths seemed impossible for the family. We decided to ask Sam, our beloved friend and the rector of our church, if he would do it for us. Without hesitation, he consented, and after he gently told them of their parents' tragedy, he drove them out to my parents' home where our family had gathered, anxiously awaiting their arrival.

I can remember watching the four of them—Sam and the three little girls—as they entered the front door of the family home. We all wondered about the extent of the girls' understanding of the fatal event, but what distracted us from the pain of our grief as we stood around watching remains etched in my memory. Sam carefully sat down, cross-legged, in the middle of the living room floor, and the three little girls sat around him. With paper and scissors in hand, he amazed and entertained them as he cut out the most beautiful chain of paper dolls I had ever seen. There he was, a minister of the church dressed in a dark gray suit and clerical collar, sitting on the floor, playing with the little girls. In that tragic moment, his sensitivity and compassion ministered to us all.

Age doesn't seem to matter to God. And I'm beginning to wonder whether events do. I believe what does matter to God is that we allow Him to be with us and heal us as we cut around the dark times when we walk through the valley of the shadow of death.

"But a certain Samaritan, who was on a journey, came upon him; and when he saw him, he felt compassion."
Luke 10:33

Hoping for Glory

Christ in you!
Who me?
Yes you!
So hard to hear, embrace, believe!

Can I really be that person?
Do I really believe:
The Holy Spirit within has the power
to change me and mold me,
into that lovely creature
I was created to be?

Yes!
I can be unique,
pure, consistent
and committed!

The question is:
Will I?
Will I be Christ to others?
For His sake?

 here's responsibility there! Knowing that His Spirit lives in me, calling me to be different. Once I heard it described something like this: "Being unique makes an impression. Being pure provides a standard. Being consistent gives us stability. Being committed gives us direction."

It sounds impossible! I once complained to my sister-in-law how difficult it was to avoid being swept up by society's demands that cause me to leave God's work of love undone.

"You have to keep your eyes on Jesus," she said gently. I cupped my hands around my eyes and thought of the blinders racehorses wear that force them to look straight ahead toward their goal. Then I remembered Paul's words in his letter to the Philippian church: "I press on toward the goal for the prize of the upward call of God in Christ Jesus" (Phil. 3:14).

Wilma was a hospice patient I visited weekly for the last three months of her life. She was one who wore such blinders, never wanting to take her eyes off Jesus as she drew nearer to her death. My visits as chaplain were very important to her. She was eager for me to remind her of all the ways God loved her.

My assignment from her each week was to research the Scriptures to discover God's promises to His children. Every time I entered her bedroom she would greet me with a big smile and, with expectancy in her voice, would ask about my findings. Because I never wanted to disappoint her, I worked hard researching them. Week after week we would track them together in our Bibles, then discuss them until we felt we understood their meaning for us.

Wilma taught me a lot about intercessory prayer. She asked how she could pray for my family, and those specific requests were written down in a spiral notebook along with many others that had been given to her. She prayed for each daily. And even when she became too weak to say each name, her daughter gently placed the notebook upon her chest, believing that the Lord knew and honored her intent. That was the way she died one Sunday morning.

I believe Wilma was unique. As I think back on my time spent with her, I realize the impact she had on my life. Her purity of heart was apparent to her family and friends. She stayed consistent to the end in her desire to learn and internalize the Word of

God. There was never a question in her mind of her commitment to the Christ she knew and loved as Lord, believing that even those who are dying can bring a wholeness to those they leave behind.

Christ in you, the hope of glory.
Colossians 1:27

Seasons

Lift high the cross!
I am not able.
Folks rush past me
in order to follow you, Lord.
They brush past me
not even recognizing my woundedness.
They see me as a fellow warrior,
and yet
I feel limp, hungry, thirsty.
They move past
expecting me to be a part
of The Great March.
They don't see.
They don't know,
except for one or two to whom
I've shown my hollow self.

Lift high Your cross,
so that I may see to follow.
Cause some to linger by my side.
To dress my wounds.
To stand me up.
To help me walk.
I must walk first.
Then I'll march.
I know I can!
I know I will!
You wait and see.

 he death of my mother helped me get in touch with my feelings of loss in a way I had never done before. As I began to reflect on that which transpired within me during her last few months of life upon this earth, I likened it to one of my scuba diving adventures opening up a whole new world of reality for me.

As Mother's life came to an end, it was as if I was surfacing from a deep dive and could see the light of day from underneath where I had been submerged for a long time.

Being a diver, I know the beauty that lies beneath the watery surface. Many times, fearful of the unknown world below me, I've nervously taken the plunge, diving downward into the depths, then landing upon the ocean's soft floor only to discover the beauty of a whole other world—a world that can only be experienced by becoming dependent upon another source for life's support.

Although I did not want to walk down the path of death with my mother, within the depths of that bittersweet adventure I discovered incredible beauty in life that defies my attempt of description. No striving of my own could bring me up from the depths of the emotional pain she and I shared. When I realized this I began to live in the flow of the death current that was slowly taking Mother away, and I discovered that I was being swept along beautiful new vistas of life I never knew existed. Her dying was spiced with newfound love and profound joy.

As the Old Testament writer said, there really is a season and a time for everything under the sun! There is a time for dying to be born anew. I know now that God was the life support that kept me moving through the current of sad passings. Through friends, He helped me realize the importance of staying a part of other lives when I would have preferred to pull inward into myself. Through them, His love nurtured and encouraged me. In His mysterious, holy, unique way He brought the strength of joy and a peace that defied explanation to my grieving heart.

There is an appointed time for everything. . . .
A time to give birth, and a time to die. . . .
Ecclesiastes 3:1–2

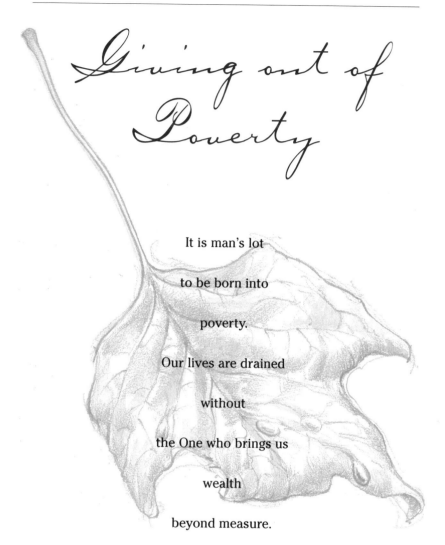

Giving out of Poverty

It is man's lot

to be born into

poverty.

Our lives are drained

without

the One who brings us

wealth

beyond measure.

 s my mother's life moved to its earthly close, God in His mercy revealed to me a deep well of poverty within myself I can only describe as a poor ability to demonstrate my love for my mother.

As I listened to her share her feelings about dying, naming regrets about coming events she wouldn't be around to experience, I felt a great tug at my heart. I watched the destruction of the cancer as it progressed over that year and the effect it had on her facial appearance. She had been a young and vital eighty-five-year-old when the disease began. A year later, on her eighty-sixth birthday she said to me, "Are you sure that I'm not turning ninety-six instead?" Even though she was trying to find some humor in the tragedy, it weighed heavily on my heart.

About a year before she died, I was reading a story in the Gospel of Mark about the widow's mite. I kept rereading the verse: "For they all put in out of their surplus, but she, out of her poverty" (12:44).

I stopped to reflect upon what form my own poverty took. I remember being puzzled. What disguise does my poverty wear? I asked myself. Certainly, materially speaking, I wasn't poor. Yet, deep down inside I knew there existed a deep and ugly pocket of poverty, and I also knew it was God who drew my attention to it. So in my prayer time, I sought His help. What He revealed to me sounded something like this: "Bitsy, you are poor in the ways you show your love for your mother."

The truth hit hard. I had always felt inadequate. There never had been a spontaneity of love between us, yet I don't believe we ever doubted its existence. A loving touch or a spoken word of love were seldom a part of my childhood. I can't recall words of encouragement and affirmation. Hugs and kisses were the exception and not the rule. So I concluded that what I had never received from her, I did not know how to give back in return. I was poor indeed! I knew it, and I was saddened by the truth.

But God never leaves us helpless. In response to that painful revelation, I prayed to Jesus asking that He help me give Mother the love she needed in a way that would enable her to feel it and believe in it. In my journal that morning I wrote, "Help me to give out of my poverty, Lord."

A few weeks later an opportunity presented itself. The radiation treatments to Mother's throat had caused her to become malnourished and dehydrated. Growing weak, she collapsed and had to be hospitalized. This extremely independent woman had become frightened and helpless. She became the object of my new and sometimes awkward demonstrations of affection and patience as I rushed to give her the physical and emotional support she needed. It grew much easier for me to speak reassuring and loving words she so desperately needed to hear.

And Mother gave too. Out of her poverty flowed increasing gifts of affection toward me as the weeks wore on and the disease ravaged her body. She watched me come and go, spending most of my time meeting her daily needs. I knew that it was difficult for her to accept so much of my help, even though she knew she was unable to do for herself.

She experienced my giving in a way she never had before, and that blessed her. As I walked into her room on the morning of my birthday, she gave me the best gift ever of her life. Rising up out of her favorite chair, she pulled me to herself and said, "Oh, you are a wonderful daughter, and I do love you!" In that moment I realized that the old, deep pocket of poverty inside me had been transformed into a deep well of life-giving water. It had been born of Christ's Spirit.

Is it too painful for you to look inside your impoverished soul? I believe there was great rejoicing in heaven when I chose to ask that I be able to see inside myself, and even greater joy when I began to give from that emptiness within. Wonder of wonders—as I continue to draw from what was originally revealed to be empty, it has never gone dry!

And a poor widow came and put in two small copper coins,
which amount to a cent. And calling His disciples to Him,
He said to them, "Truly I say to you,
this poor widow put in more than all the contributors to the
treasury; for they all put in out of their surplus,
but she, out of her poverty,
put in all she owned, all she had to live on."
Mark 12:42–44

Coming and Going

On radiant streams of glory,

out of the history of mankind

come with fury,

come with splendor,

hearts are waiting,

O Ancient of Days

come.

You who sit enthroned in glory,

make Yourself known.

Come into the present,

come into this moment,

You Eternal, Ancient of Days,

come!

 will never forget my first visit to Bernice's tiny home. I was shown into her bedroom by Anna, one of her adult daughters. Bernice lay in a bed surrounded by crucifixes and pictures of Jesus. I was the hospice chaplain who had gone to pay a visit, hoping to help her through the difficult task of dying.

She was a simple and pleasant woman, and as often as I visited her, I never heard her complain about the pain she had or the fact that she was dying. It was her children who complained. They didn't express sad feelings at the thought of losing their mother. They just talked about how they were convinced she wasn't saved. So their complaining was about her faith, or the lack of it, as they thought the case to be.

"She doesn't know Scripture," they would tell me. They wanted to remove her crucifixes and rosary. They wanted to take down her pictures of Jesus. Their newly embraced form of Christianity couldn't allow for the ancient symbols of a church that had endured the centuries. However, as an outsider, I saw in Bernice the faithful and trusting heart of a child. It was true that she couldn't quote Scripture, but the name of her Savior, Jesus Christ, was often on her lips.

"Don't lose heart over your mother's faith," I said to her children one day as they gathered outside her bedroom door. "I believe she knows her Lord," I added truthfully, hoping to comfort them and dispel their fear.

Reading the fourteenth chapter of the Gospel of John had brought freedom and reassurance to dying patients I visited. Bernice was no exception, and I read it to her on several occasions to remind her of our Lord's promise that He would come again to receive her to Himself. Yet I never dreamed that it would play such a tremendous role in the last few moments of her life.

The news of her death reached me later in the morning of its peaceful coming. I was told that Bernice had felt well enough the previous afternoon to help Anna cut and shred carrots for a carrot cake. But Anna had stayed by her mother's bedside through the night because she felt that Bernice had become very tired and much weaker.

"She had begun to get restless that last hour," Anna related, "and a few moments before she died, Mother told me to stand back away from her bed. I was puzzled by this strange request.

In a weak but clear voice she explained to me that Jesus was coming for her and she wanted Him to be able to reach her, so I needed to move away from the bed," Anna explained. "The next moment Mother raised her frail little arms, and looking straight ahead she said, 'Jesus! Jesus!' Then she was gone."

What an ending! I believe the last thing Bernice gave to her children was the knowledge that she was not only saved, but that she personally knew and loved her Lord Jesus and that He loved her too. To all of us who cared for her, she gave added reassurance that Christ does come and bring the ultimate healing to those who belong to Him.

One Saturday Rollins and I were doing our morning jog around the neighborhood. Since he was playing in an early golf tournament, he wasn't able to complete the forty-five minute route with me. As we neared the corner where he had to turn back toward home, he looked at me and said, "Bye. Love you."

I replied, "Have fun. Leave the door open for me."

"I will," came his final reply as he jogged up the hill toward the house.

I immediately found my mind invaded with thoughts of our own deaths—that final parting from one another. I took turns visualizing one or the other of us lying in a bed with the other one beside it. I realized that what we had just said to one another in parting is just what I would want us to say when the time comes for us to part at death.

Slowly, I repeated our last conversation as I continued jogging toward home.

"Bye. Love you," he had said.

I had responded, "Have fun. Leave the door open for me."

As Christians, we can look forward to an eternal, joy-filled life. We should remember that when we die, we will fall asleep in the Lord, to be there until His second triumphant coming. At that time we will precede our living brothers and sisters into heaven (1 Thess. 4:13–18). And I hope that Bernice will be there helping to hold the gates of heaven open for Anna and the rest of her family as they follow her into the place where there will be no more pain or sorrow.

"And if I go and prepare a place for you, I will come again, and receive you to Myself; that where I am, there you may be also."
John 14:3

The Look of Love

God's eyes aren't dulled

by my sins.

No,

His hope in me

keeps burning deep within them.

It is His flame of

love

reflected in me

that radiates

His glory.

y husband and I were anxious as we returned to the hospital. We had received a long-distance call from his mother's doctor telling us she had suffered a heart attack and was dying.

Only twelve short hours before, we had driven out of the hospital parking lot feeling optimistic about her condition. She had been admitted a week earlier for a bleeding ulcer. After a week's time she was healing well and expected to be going home soon. The heart attack certainly had caught us by surprise.

It was 11:00 P.M. We hoped that she would hold on to life until we were able to be by her side and say our good-byes. We entered the dimly lit room in the coronary care unit where she had been hastily moved a few hours before. We found her attached to a heart monitor and a pulse oximeter by way of a tiny clamp on her index finger, which glowed a bright red. Intravenous fluid and pain medicine were keeping her comfortable. Pale green lines were passing across screen monitors while intermittent beeps came from the IV monitoring machine. She lay still, her breathing labored and her eyes open. She smiled as we drew near the bed. I caught my breath as I looked at her face. She looked radiant!

"Hi, Mom," I managed to say, as I fought back tears and swallowed hard against the lump in my throat. "You look beautiful!"

She looked at me and smiled. Then, in a soft, clear voice, she simply said, "That's because you love me."

I wasn't prepared for the overwhelming sense of gratitude that flooded over me. I felt as if I had been washed by streams of living water. My mind raced back over the many times throughout the thirty-six years of our marriage that I had felt I had let her down, that I had not loved her as I should have. But in the five wonderful words she spoke, I realized she knew the truth, and the truth was, and always had been, that I loved her very much.

I believe that I saw her as God must see each one of us. For even though she was dying, I was blind to her illness because of my love for her. So, too, does God see our radiance even though we are ravaged by the ills of our sinfulness.

God loves us so much that He allowed His only Son, Jesus Christ, to die on the cross for our sins. I can't comprehend the immensity of that kind of love. I can't imagine that, in all of my imperfection, He sees me radiantly beautiful. Yet, I am a reflection of His image because I was created in His likeness

(Gen. 1:26). Do I hold myself in such esteem? Do I hold others that way too?

It would be wonderful if we could see others as He sees us and then be free enough to tell them how really beautiful they are!

> *"For God loved the world so much that*
> *he gave his only Son . . ."*
> John 3:16

Prophecy

Cold, grey days deepened

the loss of love, and

once cherished celebrations

lay in their final rest.

I felt the pain

of lost traditions.

False security in them

dulled my focus

on the true gift of joy—

Jesus!

The Christmas season following the death of my mother-in-law was depressing. My own mother had died the year before. The loss of the "last" parent left Rollins and me feeling empty as the holiday season began. I became more keenly empathetic toward the many people who experience depression every year at Christmas.

The week before Christmas Day I began to reflect on the changes that we would experience. Because of these two significant deaths, our home would not be quite the same traditional gathering place for Christmas dinner for our extended family. A deep sadness enveloped me; the days were gray, and the expectancy of a "lonely" Christmas hung heavy in the air.

But how could I complain if I truly believed that Jesus is sufficient for all my needs? I was caught up in the nostalgia of it all; the loss of significant loved ones has a way of stirring deep longing, the yearning for what once was. But change happens. Always. Some changes are good, however very often there is pain. Here it was Christmas—the celebration proclaiming Christ's birth—and I was focusing on loss, the naked truth about the pain of death—death of loved ones, of relationships, even of traditions.

Christ came into this world to free us from the sting of all death. He knew the cost of loving others would eventually bring pain. Yes, the price is high in time, energy, and trust.

But if we truly believe the price has been paid, then His resurrection and ours are assured. We can trust the Truth that we celebrate at Christmastime in a new way, for it begins our own entry into His heavenly kingdom.

That was the good news John the Baptist shouted as he came out of the wilderness! He was telling all who came within the sound of his voice about the One who was coming to set them free. It wasn't a new message. It had been delivered by the ancient prophet Isaiah centuries before. But this time, the Good News came in the form of God with skin! From within that tiny body birthed in a cow stall came the Light that would dispel all darkness and death and bring health to man's soul: the prophecy of joy to the world.

"And you, child, will be called the prophet of the Most High;
For you will go on BEFORE THE LORD TO PREPARE HIS WAYS; . . .
TO SHINE UPON THOSE WHO SIT IN DARKNESS AND THE SHADOW OF DEATH,
To guide our feet into the way of peace."
Luke 1:76, 79

Betrayal

Betrayal, then disbelief.
Hurting and frightened,
I don't know where to turn.
Inside ache so strong.
Churning feelings numb,
I lick my wounds as if I were an animal,
wounded and fearful.
I cannot trust!
Where to turn?

Into the quiet I run,
I seek You for solace.
I yearn for You to heal my hurt.
I know in some miserably insufficient way
the way You might have felt
that night.

I yearn for comfort,
aching to be loved, to be touched.
Yet I accept the cup
of betrayal extended to me
by him who called himself
"friend."

Yes!
I know You know my pain.
You hear my cry.
You answer, speaking to me
gently, quietly,
and with love.

Just one small word You speak.
Simply, with tenderness.
Just one small word,
whispered
into my mind and heart.
"Trust!"

 n Maundy Thursday of Passion Week, Christians recall Christ's night of betrayal. I reread the story of that fateful event, and I cannot imagine the feelings that

Jesus must have experienced. Neither can I imagine the feelings that Clay was experiencing as he lay dying of AIDS. It was also on a Maundy Thursday that I first met him. As the hospice chaplain, I was told that he wished to see me. I recall how hard it was to make a visit like this one. I never knew what I'd find. Nor did I ever know how patients would feel as they watched me enter their rooms. It was my job to bring comfort in their final days or hours. And sometimes I was expected to have all the answers.

Clay lived in a housing project on the west side of town. Even with that knowledge, I was unprepared for the extreme poverty stretched out before me as I brought my car to a stop alongside the curb that early spring day. I was ushered into his small apartment by a wonderfully caring lady friend and her two little children. They had come from Louisiana to care for Clay until he died.

I wasn't prepared for what I felt when I entered this dying man's room. I will never forget Clay's face. He was a black man with beautiful skin. It was as if a skilled sculptor had chiseled his face out of bronze. It was a handsome, strong face; and as I studied it, looking into his pleading eyes, I saw the face of Jesus.

Strangely, immediate anger replaced all my feelings of inadequacy. I was angry at the disease that was robbing this young man of his life as a husband and father to the loving trio who greeted me at the door. And I was angry as well that Clay, who as a young boy had chosen Christ as his Savior, long ago had turned away from Him until now. Suddenly, in a desperate attempt to regain his health, he looked imploringly for me to say the magic words that would take that insidious disease from him.

What could I say that would take away his inner pain caused by hurt and fear? What would bring him peace? Could I reassure him that his salvation had been granted him that Friday afternoon when Christ died on the cross for the sins of the world?

I don't know if Clay lived out his last few days with any sort of peace, for I realized in my time with him that his fear arose out of his desperate struggle with the results of his own betrayals: first to a life with Christ for himself and, secondly, to a family life with the three people who had met me at the door.

Times of hurt and fear sometimes come my way. It can be the result of a lack of communication with loved ones. Feelings flow strong when the tongue is unchecked and hurtful words result. Such times leave me empty and open for the enemy to assault my mind with doubts and despair. Negative self-talk has a way of turning my mind topsy, causing me to feel out of balance. Unspoken words of shame or guilt pierce and wound, and I begin to view life in a wrongful perspective. Sin has its way with me until repentance takes place!

Perhaps Clay experienced something similar. Why had he never married the lady who came to take care of him, giving his two children a legitimate father? Plans had been quickly made for a marriage to be performed, but he didn't live to have that happen. He died one day too soon. Why had his life turned topsy? Was it unfair that he was dying?

The truth of the matter is that we live in a fallen world, and life is not "fair" as we think it ought to be. We should not scream out for our rights because, as servants of the Living God, we have none. We only have a responsibility to trust in the faith we have that He will help us do the right thing in what we might call "unfair" times (Luke 17).

The story of Christ's betrayal by Judas is a poignant example. That kiss must have hurt Him deeply, and yet He was obedient to His Father's will, trusting in the incredible power of divine love. He didn't plead or argue; He just accepted the consequences and turned His eyes toward home—home to His Father by way of the cross.

I pray that before Clay died he was able to rediscover that love he once put aside—the same love that healed him as he was ushered into his eternal home.

Now he who was betraying Him gave them a sign, saying,
"Whomever I shall kiss, He is the one; seize Him."
And immediately he went to Jesus and said, "Hail Rabbi!"
and kissed Him.
Matthew 26:48–49

Good Friday

O, the devotion
and commitment
You had for Your cause!
You, precious Lord,
willing to die
so I could live.
Not complaining.
No,
not once.
Just suffering unto death
for the cause.
That sweet cause!

Jesus, teach me
that kind
of commitment
I witness by Your
willingness
to lay down Your life
for Your friends.
Help me to want to follow
Your way.
Give me a teachable spirit,
a willingness
to walk the way You walked,
to talk the way You talked
of the love
born from within the
Father-heart of God.

 n the quiet, dark stillness early one Good Friday morning, I reflected upon this day in Jesus' life— how it began, and how it finally ended. He must have known the agony that lay ahead of Him. But He went forward because He was obedient. He never missed a cue—not one single step! He walked on in that perfect rhythm down that anointed path toward the cross. This final act of so-called justice would cause darkness over the earth, scattering hundreds of bystanders to their homes to nurse feelings of anger, resentment, remorse, and disbelief.

I have often wondered what I would have done had I been there. I like to think that I would have shown Christ mercy, reaching out to Him with comforting words as He passed by. But in all honesty, I probably wouldn't have been any different from the jeering crowd who loudly shouted their consent: "Crucify Him!"

He probably wouldn't have expected me to be any other way. He even knew that Peter, the one He trusted to build His church, would deny knowing Him, even though He wished that it not be so.

How He must have longed to hold on to His life! The earth God created can be so achingly beautiful, His creatures so wondrously lovable. We're told He experienced a conflict of heart (Luke 22:42–44), yet He prepared Himself for death with each passing hour.

His obedience in carrying out His Father's will kept Him looking past the events of that tragic day, even past the next dark day, and right on into the realm of eternity where there are no dark mornings, no heavy hearts, no dread—only freedom and light.

Jesus gave the same gift to me that day. It was my choice to receive it. I can choose His freedom and light for today, tomorrow, and all the days to follow by continuing to focus on Him.

Jesus is the only One who through God's great mercy heals my heart, mind, and soul.

"Come, you who are blessed of My Father, inherit the kingdom prepared for you from the foundation of the world."
Matthew 25:34

Epilogue

Along the Highway

As we read the Scriptures, we are reminded that down through the centuries God spoke to His children through dreams and visions. And if we believe Him to be the same yesterday, today, and forever, then we can look forward to the same revelations.

I know God has often spoken to me through dreams, but only once can I remember with great clarity how He spoke to me through a vision. Proverbs 29:18 states that where people have no vision, they perish. I interpret that as meaning that a vision from God acts like a beacon of light shining on the path He desires me to walk. Without His light, I walk in darkness.

The following story is a vision that came to me while I was meditating on the Word of God with a group of fellow Christians, and it is in the light of its truth that I measure my ministry in Christ.

There I was, standing alongside the guardrail of the median on the interstate. Traffic was whizzing by, paying no particular attention to me, even though I must have been a strange sight!

I felt in no particular danger of being struck down by the oncoming traffic, but I did feel constrained, certainly, within the median of that eight-lane highway.

Then Christ appeared up ahead of me. I thought to myself that it was just like Him to be there, as He's always with me wherever I am! When I saw Him, He stretched out His hand, extending to me the invitation to take it. I did, and somehow we walked down that noisy, busy freeway for a distance, above the frantic flow of an endless stream of cars. Just being in His company took all my fear away.

Then, for some unknown reason, He reached behind Himself with His other hand to get something. For a brief moment I was puzzled, unable to understand what He was doing. Then He held out a lunch box to me, and above the roar of the traffic I distinctly heard Him say, "Feed My sheep."

The vision was over as quickly as it had begun, and I came back into the present moment, out of that meditation, trying to make some sense of all that seemed so real. Part of me was amused by what I had just experienced. Certainly I had not walked with Christ down a grassy slope nor beside still waters. Nor had there been gentle breezes to refresh or birds singing their melodies to delight our senses. Hardly so! There we were in the midst of heavy traffic on a hot day, watching all those on the highway of life, rushing to who knows where. And in all of that frantic coming and going, He asked me to feed His sheep!

That's where I was, and He met me there. Actually, He placed me there with all good intention, not in a peaceful space, but in the fast lane where most of life is lived.

"Feed My sheep." Once more those words echo clearly in my mind. Softly I speak to Him as I would to a friend:

Lord, grant me the grace to stand by and wait for those who will pull over and stop along the journey, to take nourishment. Give me the courage to extend a hand and give them the food of life, which is the knowledge of You and Your abundant love and mercy. Help me to help them come to that still place where all of the traffic of life will cease, and You will meet them Yourself, to point them to The Way, and The Truth, and The Life.

Jesus said to him, "I am the way, and the truth, and the life; no one comes to the Father, but through Me."
John 14:6

About the Author

Bitsy Ayres Rubsamen has been actively involved in Christian work for over twenty-five years. Though a lifelong member of the Episcopal church, a conversion experience to Jesus Christ changed her attitude and the direction of her already busy adult life. Her commitment to her local church has included being an adult Bible study teacher and vestryman. She has served on the diocesan level, as well, including the establishment of the Hope for the Hungry committee, which widened her vision of the plight of the poor among the inner city, the Navajo Indians of Arizona, and her neighbors in Mexico.

No stranger to volunteerism, she was an active member of the Junior League and served as its president. She also served as one of the founding staff members of Hospice San Antonio, the first independent nonprofit hospice in the area, where she acted in a variety of capacities, including chaplain. For nine years she served as a member of the Board of Trustees of Trinity Episcopal School for Ministry, an Episcopal seminary in Ambridge, Pennsylvania, and is now serving on the Board of Trustees of Texas Military Institute, an Episcopal-owned secondary college preparatory school.

She is a native of San Antonio, where she lives with her husband, Rollins. They have a son, a married daughter, and two granddaughters. Currently she is active as a speaker, prayer minister, and spiritual director for her church.

She loves to share her faith in Jesus Christ whenever she has an opportunity.

Also available from
Broadman & Holman

Secret Life of the Soul - J. Keith Miller

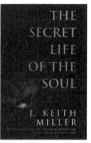

From the author of *The Taste of New Wine*, *The Secret Life of the Soul* is a journey into the innermost reaches of personal experience, where "we do our serious worrying, trying to figure things out." Spiritual problems, suggests J. Keith Miller, are the result of two parts of us— our soul and our "shaming voices"—waging a hidden internal war over our worth as a person. By shining the light of his own experience into the secret domains of the soul, Miller leads us on a search for the truth about our spiritual life.   0-8054-6375-5

The Sacred Path to Contentment - Ken Stephens

The forces of religion today are making dramatic advances, gaining church growth and political power. Yet the inner life of the modern Christian continues to lose intensity and conviction. This book, compact in size but rich in substance, is a collection of devotional thoughts. Originally written and published in France, these profound ideas are expressed with sincerity and love, and will encourage all Christians to nurture and discipline their inner life.   0-8054-0199-7

A Cup of Coffee at the Soul Cafe - Leonard Sweet

The world is becoming increasingly complicated; technology, terrorism, and disease are just some of the dangers threatening the physical and spiritual health of our modern society. For years, Leonard Sweet has been confronting these common fears in his profound and insightful series of publications, Sweet's SoulCafe. Now, in his newest book, Sweet carries the readers on a journey into the heart of spirituality, teaching Christians how to be more susceptible to God's shaping hand. *A Cup of Coffee of SoulCafe* nourishes our thirsting souls with wisdom, gently reminding us of our divine purpose.   0-8054-0159-8

Not My Will but Thine - Brenda Poinsett

Before his ministry began, Jesus knew that his purpose in life would lead to a painful death on the cross. Likewise, every Christian must face undesirable, unchangeable afflictions. The nature of God's will is often difficult to understand. Why must there be poverty? Disease? Divorce? Death? Fruitless searching for answers to these questions leads some Christians to lose all hope. *Not My Will but Thine* shows how to find comfort in God's divine plan through strong faith and intense prayer.   0-8054-6369-0

Available at fine bookstores everywhere.

Endnotes

1. Macrina Wiederkehr, *Seasons of Your Heart: Prayers and Reflection*, revised and expanded (New York: Harper Collins, 1991), 71.

2. Theodore P. Ferris, *His Holy Fellowship* (New York: The Woman's Auxiliary to the National Council), 16.

3. Brennan Manning, *The Ragamuffin Gospel* (Sisters, Ore.: Multnomah Books, 1990), 175.

4. Richard J. Foster, *Celebration of Discipline* (San Francisco: Harper & Row, 1978), 95.

5. Glenn Clark, *I Will Lift up Mine Eyes* (Eversham, Worchester: Arthur James Limited, The Drift, 1974), 38.

6. Frederick Buechner, *Wishful Thinking: A Seeker's ABC* (San Fransisco: Harper San Fransisco, 1993), 119.

7. Jeff Cothran, "Glorious in Majesty." Copyright GIA Publications, 1972. Used by permission.

8. Joan D. Chittister, *Wisdom Distilled from the Daily: Living the Rule of St. Benedict Today* (San Francisco: Harper & Row, 1990), 50.

9. Carlo Carretto, *Letters from the Desert* (Maryknoll, N.Y: Orbis Books, 1972), x.

10. Thomas Merton, *New Seeds of Contemplation* (New York: New Directions Publishing Corporation, 1972), 80.

11. Ibid., 81.